Lecture Notes in Computer Science 15175

Founding Editors

Gerhard Goos
Juris Hartmanis

W0055422

Editorial Board Members

The series Lecture Notes in Computer Science (LNCS), including its subseries Lecture Notes in Artificial Intelligence (LNAI) and Lecture Notes in Bioinformatics (LNBI), has established itself as a medium for the publication of new developments in computer science and information technology research, teaching, and education.

LNCS enjoys close cooperation with the computer science R & D community, the series counts many renowned academics among its volume editors and paper authors, and collaborates with prestigious societies. Its mission is to serve this international community by providing an invaluable service, mainly focused on the publication of conference and workshop proceedings and postproceedings. LNCS commenced publication in 1973.

Mike Preuss · Agata Leszkiewicz ·
Jean-Christopher Boucher · Ofer Fridman ·
Lucas Stampe
Editors

Disinformation in Open Online Media

6th Multidisciplinary International Symposium, MISDOOM 2024
Münster, Germany, September 2–4, 2024
Proceedings

 Springer

Editors
Mike Preuss
Leiden University
Leiden, The Netherlands

Agata Leszkiewicz
University of Twente
Enschede, The Netherlands

Jean-Christopher Boucher
University of Calgary
Calgary, AB, Canada

Ofer Fridman
King's College London
London, UK

Lucas Stampe
University of Münster
Münster, Germany

ISSN 0302-9743   ISSN 1611-3349 (electronic)
Lecture Notes in Computer Science
ISBN 978-3-031-71209-8   ISBN 978-3-031-71210-4 (eBook)
https://doi.org/10.1007/978-3-031-71210-4

Preface

Disinformation - especially in online media - is an ever-present, publicly and politically discussed topic. Targeted misinformation is an important social issue, especially in this year, which is characterized by decisive democratic elections in Europe and the US. At the same time, global conflicts and wars are always a battle for the sovereignty of information interpretation and the claim to truth.

Research, politics, journalism, and many other social actors are struggling to find solutions to detect and regulate disinformation campaigns and fakes or to understand what effects disinformation has on recipients and society. Their opponents are interest groups that use modern information technology and insights into human psychology and behavior to effectively disseminate (dis)information on a massive scale.

This year's Multidisciplinary International Symposium on Disinformation in Open Online Media (MISDOOM) is thus more relevant than ever in this field of tension. It offers scientists, journalists, NGOs and other social actors a unique forum for exchanging views on current technological, social, and regulatory topics in the research field of disinformation. Traditionally, the symposium tries to integrate the scientific process of multiple communities and offers a proceedings publication track as well as the submission of presentation proposals (as extended abstracts). The current volume gathers the full papers submitted to MISDOOM 2024.

This year's proceedings volume contains the papers accepted at the sixth edition of the symposium, organized in 2024. Like the previous successful conference in Amsterdam, MISDOOM 2024 was held in person on September 2–4, 2024 in Münster, Germany. Overall, there were 50 submissions: 15 papers and 35 extended abstracts. Reviews were single-blind. Each extended abstract was reviewed by at least two program committee members. Each paper was reviewed by at least three program committee members. The program committee decided to accept 8 paper submissions in the full paper track for publication in this LNCS volume. In addition, a total of 29 extended abstract contributions were accepted for presentation at the symposium.

We want to express our gratitude to all authors and those who contributed to organizing and running this conference. This includes the international Program Committee, the MISDOOM Steering Committee, our funders - the German Research Foundation and the Federal Ministry of Research and Education - and our sponsor: the European Research Center for Information Systems (ERCIS).

September 2024

Christian Grimme
Thorsten Quandt

Organization

General Chairs

Grimme, Christian   University of Münster, Germany
Quandt, Thorsten   University of Münster, Germany

Program Committee Chairs

Preuss, Mike   Leiden University, The Netherlands
Leszkiewicz, Agata   University of Twente, The Netherlands
Boucher, Jean-Christopher   University of Calgary, Canada
Fridman, Ofer   King's College London, UK

Programm Committee/Reviewers

Abumansour, Amani   Queen Mary University of London, UK
Adeodato, Jorge Jr.   Universidade Federal de Pernambuco, Brazil
Alizadeh, Meysam   University of Zurich, Switzerland
Assenmacher, Dennis   GESIS - Leibniz-Institut für Sozialwissenschaften, Germany
Beseler, Arista   University of Passau, Germany
Bianchi, John   IMT School for Advanced Studies Lucca, Italy
Bodenmuller, Luiza   Universidade Federal de Minas Gerais, Brazil
Clos, Jeremie   University of Nottingham, UK
Cresci, Stefano   National Research Council (IIT-CNR), Pisa, Italy
Dierickx, Laurence   University of Bergen, Norway
George, Anna   University of Oxford, UK
Grimme, Christian   University of Münster, Germany
Grimme, Britta   Paderborn University, Germany
Kessling, Philipp   Hans-Bredow-Institut, Germany
Kojan, Lilian   RWTH Aachen University, Germany
Lütke Stockdiek, Janina   University of Münster, Germany
Martinez Pandiani, Delfina Sol   CWI Amsterdam, The Netherlands
Mthethwa, Sthembile   Council for Scientific and Industrial Research, South Africa
Nieubuurt, Joshua   Old Dominion University, USA

Contents

Striking the Balance in Using LLMs for Fact-Checking: A Narrative
Literature Review 1
   Laurence Dierickx, Arjen van Dalen, Andreas L. Opdahl,
   and Carl-Gustav Lindén

Leveraging Large Language Models for Fact-Checking Farsi News
Headlines 16
   Shirin Dehghani, Mohammadmasiha Zahedivafa, Zahra Baghshahi,
   Darya Zare, Sara Yari, Zeynab Samei, Mohammadhadi Aliahmadi,
   Mahdis Abbasi, Sara Mirzamojtahedi, Sarvenaz Ebrahimi,
   and Meysam Alizadeh

Conspiracy Detection Beyond Text: Exploring the Feasibility of Adding
Psycho-Linguistic Features to Enhance Conspiracy Detection Models 32
   Anna R. George, Maximilian Ahrens, Janet B. Pierrehumbert,
   and Michael McMahon

To Share or Not to Share: Randomized Controlled Study of Misinformation
Warning Labels on Social Media 46
   Anatoliy Gruzd, Philip Mai, and Felipe B. Soares

Crowdsourcing Statement Classification to Enhance Information Quality
Prediction 70
   Jaspreet Singh, Michael Soprano, Kevin Roitero, and Davide Ceolin

The Spread of Anti-vaccination Memes on Facebook 86
   Aleksi Knuutila, Anna George, Jonathan Bright, Kate Joynes-Burgess,
   and Philip Howard

Multi-platform Framing Analysis: A Case Study of Kristiansand Quran
Burning 101
   Anna-Katharina Jung, Gautam Kishore Shahi, Jennifer Fromm,
   Kari Anne Røysland, and Kim Henrik Gronert

Understanding Political Communication and Polarisation: A Case Study
of the Colombian President's X Utilisation 131
   María José González-Méndez and Niklas Kloth

x   Contents

Correction to: The Spread of Anti-vaccination Memes on Facebook C1
  Aleksi Knuutila, Anna George, Jonathan Bright, Kate Joynes-Burgess,
  and Philip Howard

Author Index   147

Striking the Balance in Using LLMs for Fact-Checking: A Narrative Literature Review

Laurence Dierickx[1,2(✉)] ⓘ, Arjen van Dalen[2] ⓘ, Andreas L. Opdahl[1] ⓘ,
and Carl-Gustav Lindén[1] ⓘ

[1] Department of Information Science and Media Studies, University of Bergen,
Bergen, Norway
Laurence.Dierickx@uib.no

[2] Digital Democracy Centre, University of Southern Denmark, Odense, Denmark

Abstract. The launch of ChatGPT at the end of November 2022 triggered a general reflection on its benefits for supporting fact-checking workflows and practices. Between the excitement of the availability of AI systems that no longer require the mastery of programming skills and the exploration of a new field of experimentation, academics and professionals foresaw the benefits of such technology. Critics have raised concerns about the fairness and of the data used to train Large Language Models (LLMs), including the risk of artificial hallucinations and the proliferation of machine-generated content that could spread misinformation. As LLMs pose ethical challenges, how can professional fact-checking mitigate risks? This narrative literature review explores the current state of LLMs in the context of fact-checking practice, highlighting three key complementary mitigation strategies related to education, ethics and professional practice.

Keywords: Fact-checking · Large Language Models · Risk mitigation

1 Introduction

The launch of ChatGPT on 30 November 2022 marked a significant milestone in the integration of artificial intelligence (AI) into newsrooms [1]. Its user-friendly interface and the elimination of the need for extensive programming skills accelerated this process [2]. Building on the success of the Generative Pre-trained Transformer (GPT) architecture, Large Language Models (LLMs) such as Chat-GPT use machine learning on large databases to generate content [3,4]. As foundational models, LLMs operate by learning patterns and information from vast datasets, which presents complexities in ensuring ethical use and reliable results in fact-checking, although they are seen as an opportunity to improve workflows and augment professional practice [5–7].

Ethical concerns arise from the opacity of data collection and training datasets, where biased and inaccurate data can skew results [8,9]. For instance,

M. Preuss et al. (Eds.): MISDOOM 2024, LNCS 15175, pp. 1–15, 2024.
https://doi.org/10.1007/978-3-031-71210-4_1

studies have shown that ChatGPT's primary sources are not immune to bias, error or partisanship [10–12]. Its use of copyrighted data increases the risk of plagiarism, as the system tends to reproduce sentences from its training dataset [13]. Another significant challenge lies in its potential to spread misinformation and disinformation [14,15]. Because LLMs generate content that is not easily distinguishable from human-generated information, they are potentially harmful tools [16]. However, the generation of misleading content is not always intentional and also includes artificial hallucinations, a well-known problem, which refers to the generation of fact-like claims that contradict real-world facts [17,18]. Further, the black-box nature of LLMs raises questions of trustworthiness and accountability, exacerbating existing concerns about AI and generative artificial intelligence (GAI) [19–22].

Given the ethical challenges and limitations of these technologies, what is the potential for professional fact-checking, and how can the risks be mitigated? This paper addresses this question through a narrative literature review; a qualitative research tool used strategically to allow flexibility in exploring different methodologies. Its primary aim is to provide a comprehensive overview of existing knowledge in an emerging field [23–25]. This research builds on previous related research, which consist of a systematic review of automated fact-checking from an end-user perspective [26] and a study on dealing with factuality in LLMs [27]. The paper collection is essentially based on a snowball method, a technique in which initial sources lead the researcher to further relevant studies. This iterative and qualitative approach facilitated the exploration of recent advances in LLMs in journalism studies and information science. In this research, fact-checking is approached as a specialised sub-genre of journalism that fulfils the promise of objective and responsible reporting [28,29].

To provide an in-depth understanding of the topic, this paper is divided into two main sections: (1) outlining the contours of professional fact-checking by describing its processes and exploring its intersection with technology, and (2) examining the potential applications of LLMs in fact-checking and formulating strategies for effectively mitigating the risks. To highlight the implications associated with LLMs in fact-checking, this study adopts an interdisciplinary approach [30]. We identified three complementary strategies: education through AI literacy, ethics through promoting human oversight to ensure accountability, and professional practice through improving prompt engineering the instructions provided by the user to the system– to achieve better results.

2   Fact-Checkers and Fact-Checking Technology

In journalism, verification is an ethical standard ensuring the reliability, accuracy, credibility and truthfulness of the news [31–33]. Verification takes place before publication, whereas fact-checking takes place after publication. It has evolved as a sub-genre in journalism, following the need to verify political discourses and the content propagated on social media [34,35]. In practice, fact-checking is an iterative and time-consuming process that can be standardised into five main stages. These stages are well documented in the literature, particularly in discussions of automated fact-checking techniques [36, 37].

1. **Media monitoring:** This stage involves actively monitoring various social media platforms and political sources to identify claims or statements needing verification or worth checking [38]. Monitoring tasks can be supported by AI technology, as it is time-consuming when performed manually [39].
2. **Selecting the claim to check:** Fact-checkers decide which claims or information to check based on relevance, potential impact and other criteria. This stage primarily requires critical thinking skills and mandates that fact-checkers also question their possible selection bias [40, 41]. Machine learning and natural language applications can be used in this process, for claim detection or claim selection, including assessing the newsworthiness of the claim [42–44].
3. **Verification and evidence gathering:** Verification aims to assess the truth, accuracy or validity of a claim [33]. For this, fact-checkers thoroughly investigate selected claims, using traditional journalistic methods such as expert interviews, digital tools and open-source information to gather evidence. The techniques and methods used depend on the nature of the claim being verified, whether it is textual or audiovisual. Verification of social media content is particularly challenging as it involves the assessment of user-generated content, which has greater potential for manipulation, alteration and removal from context [35]. This stage of the process can be supported by a wide range of digital tools, of which the AI-based ones are mostly concerned with assigning credibility ratings to information [35, 45].
4. **Giving a verdict:** Based on the evidence collected, fact-checkers determine the accuracy of the claim and assign a verdict, such as "True", "False" or "Misleading". The rating used may differ from one fact-check to another, and may also differ when the same claim is fact-checked by two different organisations [46]. Recognising the possibility of nuances between truth and falsehood, some fact-checking organisations have developed a rating scale, but this can be difficult to use at the operational level [47]. Machine learning predictive algorithms are likely to support this stage [42, 44, 48].
5. **Producing the narrative:** The final stage involves articulating the findings and evidence comprehensively and communicating them to audiences through articles, reports or other content. Transparent storytelling is rooted in open-source practices and involves the integration of digital skills and visual evidence collected during the investigation. As such, fact-checkers not only present facts but also reveal the methods used in fact-checking [49]. This stage could be assisted by natural language generation methods, but we did not find any evidence of effective use in the literature review.

2.1 From Traditional to Technological Skills

Technological advances aim to support fact-checking practices in a process that is acknowledged as being time-consuming. They unfold in a context where journalists have always had an ambivalent relationship with technology. While they are open to technologies that benefit their work, they balance technological opportunities and challenges with their professional autonomy and identity [50–52].

The adoption of technologies in journalism is influenced by a multifaceted interplay of socio-professional factors, including professional backgrounds, individual skills, and organisational contexts [53]. A recent study in Norway revealed a nuanced integration of fact-checking into journalism, highlighting the tension between preserving traditional skills and embracing innovative methods. Notably, fact-checkers in the study relied increasingly on digital verification tools [54]. Swedish newsrooms face analogous challenges in navigating organisational dynamics, time constraints, and barriers to skills acquisition [55].

Verifying the accuracy of sources and content is particularly complex in the dynamic landscape of social media platforms, where user-generated content often serves as a conduit for misinformation and disinformation [35]. The complexity escalates with the potential for misrepresentation when critical context is omitted [56]. The application of open source intelligence (OSINT) methods and tools, which leverage publicly available resources such as geolocation data, facial recognition technology, and web archives, has significant potential to revolutionize investigative techniques by enhancing accuracy and depth of analysis through the integration of digital tools [49,57,58]. Despite their potential benefits, fact-checkers have not yet widely adopted OSINT methods due to a lack of awareness and skills in using such tools [40]. More generally, fact-checkers often rely on familiar tools for research and verification, despite the plethora of digital tools at their disposal [53,59].

Developing a critical mindset coupled with logical reasoning remains one of the fundamental skills for fact-checkers [53], distinguishing human judgement from automated systems [60]. Emotional and social intelligence, essential for nuanced journalistic judgement, cannot be replicated in computer code; AI-based systems may mimic human patterns but do not possess human understanding [61]. Therefore, integrating technological innovation in journalism and fact-checking is a complex issue, influenced more by social and cultural considerations than mere technical advances. Furthermore, concerns remain about the potential of technology to compromise professional autonomy [62], underscoring the need for preserving human agency and professional values [52,63,64].

2.2 Practices of Transparency vs. Opacity of Technology

AI-based technologies challenge ethical fact-checking practices in a number of ways. The majority of European fact-checking organisations typically adhere to a newsroom model, where teams operate under journalistic standards centred on truthfulness, fairness and accuracy [65,66]. Their professional identity also depends on a strong commitment to transparency, particularly among those who belong to the International Fact-Checking Network (IFCN) or the European Fact-Checking Standards Networks (EFSCN). Membership of these networks mandates transparency about sources, funding, methods and correction policies, thereby aligning journalistic ethics with accountability standards [53]. However, not all fact-checkers prioritise transparency as their primary professional norm, privileging accuracy, impartiality, objectivity or independence instead [28].

Fact-checkers whose organisations are signatories to the IFCN standards are granted access to Facebook's third-party fact-checking programme, consisting of a tool that facilitates the identification of checkworthy viral content. The reliance of Facebook's algorithm on an opaque process and lack of accountability for its behaviour does not prevent its use, although fact-checkers have criticised its opacity [53]. This is usually the case when fact-checkers use technology: it is not common for systems to be documented for their end users, and fact-checkers often lack awareness of the technological intricacies that underpin their functionality [67]. This highlights the critical role of explainability in AI-based technologies, which aims to increase trust and reliability by understanding the reasoning behind outcomes [10]. In AI ethics, explainability complements transparency as it also helps to assign responsibility for unintended consequences [68]. While explainability does not ensure trustworthy AI, it is a critical tool for fostering trust in AI [69,70]. This need for accountability is particularly evident in automated fact-checking technology, where concerns about trust and algorithmic accountability remain significant barriers to widespread adoption [71].

The limited adoption of computational tools by fact-checkers is not only due to transparency issues, but also to their specialisation in specific fact-checking functions, requiring manual effort and lacking seamless integration [72]. Despite advances in AI-based solutions, skepticism remains among fact-checkers, especially regarding critical processes such as contextualisation and the management of real-time constraints [67,72]. Furthermore, fact-checking technologies developed outside the field often diverge from the expertise and values of fact-checkers [26,48], whereas human-in-the-loop approaches have shown significant benefits [73,74]. This underlines that technology alone cannot adequately address the complex societal challenges posed by information disorders.

3   Use Cases for LLMs

The integration of LLMs into fact-checking practices is based on the premise that humans may struggle to manage vast amounts of disinformation [75]. In this narrative literature review, we do not distinguish between specific systems, as ChatGPT is not the only LLM available on the market. Instead, it provides a comprehensive overview of potential risks and mitigation strategies based on the current state of knowledge.

3.1   Possibilities and Identification of Risk Factors

Research has identified several ways in which AI-based technology is likely to improve fact-checking workflows and practices, recognising that verification also relies on different standards, individual judgements, first-hand experience and relationships with sources [76]. In investigative journalism, AI methods have been used to uncover hidden patterns in large amounts of data, although these efforts have produced modest results due to unique story requirements and issues of data availability and quality [77]. AI methods in fact-checking can be used for social media monitoring, assessing the newsworthiness of a claim, stance detection, searching for previous fact-checks, audiovisual content verification, semi-automated classification, feature extraction, writing tasks or disseminating fact-checks [72, 78]. Similarly, LLMs are considered to have potential for extracting data from large amounts of information, providing contextual information, detecting disinformation, analysing data, summarising text, detecting stance, writing and supporting multilingual tasks [4, 30].

In their pioneering study conducted in Spain, Cuartielles et al. identified several benefits for using LLMs in fact-checking, such as the ease of data collection and the ability of AI tools such as ChatGPT to provide synthetic and rapid information, and contextual insights for fact-checking processes [6]. The study also highlighted the potential for self-learning, improving the performance of the system and contributing to the development of more specialised tools devoted to specific tasks [6]. Practically, LLMs are likely to support each stage of the manual fact-checking process as illustrated in Table 1.

Table 1. Identifying potential for using LLMs to support the fact-checking process

Fact-Checking Stage	LLMs Associated Tasks
1. Media monitoring	Extracting data from multiple sources, including social media corpora, to create rich datasets for subsequent analysis. Processing and organising large amounts of data.
2. Selecting the claim to check	Identifying and prioritising claims for review, including providing contextual analysis to support the decision.
3. Verification and evidence gathering	Cross-referencing the identified claims with sources or databases of factual information. Preparing summaries of the information gathered. Analysing the collected data, assessing the accuracy based on the analysis.
4. Giving a verdict	Providing contextual understanding to support judgment.
5. Producing the narrative	Generating texts based on pre-defined templates. Supporting the production of clear and structured narratives.

Despite all these promises, LLMs remain untrustworthy for most practical fact-checking uses due to several current challenges, including dealing with artificial hallucinations [10,79]. Unlike intrinsic hallucinations, which contradict the content of the source, extrinsic hallucinations in a LLM cannot be verified by the source because the systems do not provide the source on which they base their results [80]. Hallucinations are a well-known phenomenon and they are explained by the fact that the system has been trained to generate maximally plausible sequences of words, not to internalise world knowledge, although research also pointed out explanations related to the use of large amounts of unsupervised data, a lack of quality in the training data and the black-box nature of the system [18,81,82]. In addition, LLMs face limitations in contextual understanding and may lack access to real-time or updated data [4,18]. Retrieval-Augmented Generation (RAG) is a technique used to combat hallucinations. It consists of augmenting the system with external data, assuming that contextual information from external sources will improve text generation [2,83]. However, this technical solution is inaccessible to fact-checkers, who can enhance their prompting techniques by providing additional information.

When dealing with long documents, summarising can lead to important context being omitted [3]. Further, there is a gap in understanding the origin of the source, with a noticeable lack of source transparency in the results generated by the system [2,6,13,68,79]. Moreover, bias in the collection and training of data remains an open issue [4,79]. Using LLMs in fact-checking also introduces several risks that demand careful considerations. These risks encompass the potential creation and dissemination of unintentional disinformation (artificial hallucinations) or intentional misinformation that is difficult to detect [10,13,84]. The confident tone of the output can also be misleading, especially since the system might misinterpret the data and have a limited understanding of technical terms [2,79]. Further, the articulate communication of LLMs can encourage a misleading tendency towards anthropomorphism-the attribution of human characteristics to the system [2]. The use of LLMs in fact-checking poses other challenges related to artificial hallucinations, which are problematic for generating expert knowledge [18], and to copyrighted data, involving a risk of plagiarism [10,13]. Another concern is the phenomenon of deskilling, already observed during previous industrial revolutions [85]. For fact-checkers, it refers to the decline in critical thinking and problem-solving skills [4,86].

The hype surrounding LLMs may have social consequences, in terms of anxiety about workforce displacements [13,87]. Further, the perceived credibility and reliability of LLMs is likely to undermine the user's trust in technology, which plays a pivotal role in shaping interactions between humans and AI systems [88–90]. Hence, fact-checkers may see LLMs as a supplementary tools rather than a means to augment human possibilities [6]. Research in this area is still nascent due to the novelty of the technology, but these early indicators show the ambivalent nature of LLMs and highlight the need for risk mitigation, to create the conditions for trustworthy fact-checking systems, a prerequisite for uses in journalism and fact-checking [91].

3.2   Strategies for Risk Mitigation

Three key strategies for mitigating the risks associated with LLMs are explored in this section: promoting AI literacy, encouraging human oversight and collaboration, and working on effective prompting techniques to combat artificial hallucinations. The focus is on formulating a comprehensive set of strategies that address the challenges and limitations of the technology, all within the context of fostering responsible and ethical use of LLMs in fact-checking.

Promoting AI Literacy. Fostering a robust understanding of AI among journalists and fact-checkers has never been more important than in the age of generative AI technology. Deuze and Beckett define AI literacy as "the knowledge and beliefs about artificial intelligence that facilitate its recognition, management and application" [92, p. 1913]. It is, therefore, not just about applications and practices but also has a strong ethical dimension. Further, a lack of AI literacy could have negative consequences [13]. Initial or ongoing training programmes can help to understand these challenges, equip professionals with the appropriate skills, develop a critical mindset to prevent further risks and prevent being fooled by the convincing tone of LLMs [2, 75, 93]. Clear guidelines are also needed in newsrooms to guide responsible use and best ethical practices, including the scope of LLMs and other GAI applications. In this context, it is noteworthy that until the launch of ChatGPT, the ethical use of AI was rather overlooked by self-regulatory bodies in Europe and news media organisations. The situation has changed rapidly with the development of LLMs, prompting a great deal of reflection that has led several newsrooms to adopt specific guidelines to manage the limitations and mitigate the risks associated more broadly with AI-based systems. In addition, two European press councils - in the UK (Impress) and Belgium (Raad voor de Journalistiek) - have already adapted their codes of journalistic ethics with an emphasis on accuracy and transparency [94].

Human Oversight and Collaboration. Maintaining human oversight to balance accuracy when there is no guarantee of algorithmic accountability is a strategy to mitigate potential adverse effects [18]. It enables fact-checkers to use LLMs for close supervision [6]. It is, therefore, also a mitigation strategy that preserves the autonomy and authority of fact-checkers, or in other words, their role in evaluating and validating claims [41]. The principle of human oversight involves collaboration with humans, according to a human-in-the-loop approach that incorporates external knowledge, tools and multimodal information augmentation. Such a collaborative approach improves accuracy, reinforces the ethical use of LLMs in journalism and fact-checking, and improves the overall user experience [95]. It is also deemed to get better results from the perspective of a human-machine association for human augmentation [10]. The majority of newsrooms that have adopted ethical guidelines for using AI and GAI have placed this principle at the forefront of their recommendations, recognising the human responsibility [94]. For fact-checkers, it can be considered a means to maintain a high level of transparency that counterbalances the opacity of the system.

Developing Prompting Techniques for Combating Hallucinations. The results produced by LLMs are often inexplicable and can be prone to artificial hallucinations. They can also give different answers to the same question [2]. Research has shown that the development and implementation of creative prompting techniques can significantly improve the explainability of these tools [75] and effectively mitigate the generation of fabricated content and artificial hallucinations [18,96]. Prompting involves programming the system using natural language, making it accessible to users without requiring extensive computer skills. It is seen as a valuable tool for improving the quality of results and can potentially revolutionise problem-solving in various domains [99]. To improve prompting, experimenting with different instructions can help to assess the quality of the outcome [96]. Incorporating specific context and expectations into the prompt can also improve the accuracy of the result [97,98]. In addition, prompting can be used to generate new prompts, allowing for self-adaptation and the potential for continuous improvement [99]. Prompting has also proven effective in detecting misinformation and disinformation, leveraging the world knowledge and inferential abilities of LLMs [30].

4   Discussion and Conclusion

This narrative literature review explored the ambivalent nature of LLMs and assessed their potential use in fact-checking, along with considering their limitations and the risks they may pose to the quality of information output. The main findings highlight the need to develop (G)AI literacy programmes tailored for fact-checkers, the importance of ensuring ethical use through a human-in-the-loop approach and the benefits of researching and developing prompting strategies to improve the quality of results, especially by addressing hallucination-related challenges.

Concerning automated fact-checking (AFC), LLMs may play a critical role in facilitating explainability. Although it does not guarantee that any AI-based system will be flawless, explainability can be seen as an instrument for fostering trust in AFC systems by providing a level of transparency consistent with the professional standards of fact-checkers and addressing criticisms about the opacity of systems [69]. Another benefit of explainability is that it aims to provide a comprehensive human-level understanding of how systems work in processes and decision-making [100]. However, achieving explanations that accurately reflect the inner workings of LLMs remains a challenging and ongoing area of research. Moreover, LLMs may never be able to explain how they work with an acceptable level of accuracy, fairness and reliability, mainly due to the question of the sources used in the generated results and the challenges of dealing with artificial hallucinations. When asked to explain their behaviour, LLMs may hallucinate explanations, forcing them to generate plausible-sounding but potentially inaccurate answers. This paper does not discuss tools to detect AI-generated text due to their inherent limitations regarding accuracy and reliability [101]. Relying solely on these tools could lead to overlooking nuanced aspects of fact-checking, such as context, intent and veracity of information. Therefore, an emphasis on content quality ensures a more holistic approach, combining the strengths of LLMs with human oversight to maintain professional standards. In addition, from a professional perspective, verifying the truthfulness of the content is more important than knowing how it was produced, especially since LLMs can be used ambivalently to inform and disinform. Further, this paper provides a comprehensive analysis of the state of the art, identifying key challenges and promising solutions that require further investigation. It paves the way for future empirical research to assess the effectiveness of these mitigation strategies. It also encourages a thorough assessment of the benefits and risks of using LLMs for fact-checking and, more broadly, for journalism, recognising that neither transparency nor accountability is sufficient to meet the ethical requirement of respect for facts.

Acknowledgments. This research was funded by EU CEF Grant No. 101158604.

Disclosure of Interests. The authors have no competing interests to declare that are relevant to the content of this article.

References

1. Beckett, C., Yaseen, M.: Generating Change. A global survey of what news organisations are doing with AI (2023). https://static1.squarespace.com/static/64d60527c01ae7106f2646e9. Accessed 22 June 2024
2. Augenstein, I., et al.: Factuality challenges in the era of large language models. arXiv preprint arXiv:2310.05189 (2023)
3. Aydin, Ö., Karaarslan, E.: Is ChatGPT leading generative AI? What is beyond expectations? Acad. Platform J. Eng. Smart Syst. **11**(3), 118–134 (2023)
4. Yenduri, G., et al.: GPT (Generative pre-trained transformer)-a comprehensive review on enabling technologies, potential applications, emerging challenges, and future directions. arXiv, Eprint: arXiv:2305.10435v2 (2023)
5. Unver, H.A.: Emerging Technologies and Automated Fact-Checking: Tools, Techniques and Algorithms (2023). SSRN: https://ssrn.com/abstract=4555022
6. Cuartielles, R., Ramon-Vegas, X., Pont-Sorribes, C.: Retraining fact-checkers: the emergence of ChatGPT in information verification. Profesional de la información/Inf. Profess. **32**(5) (2023)
7. Wolfe, R., Mitra, T.: The impact and opportunities of generative AI in fact-checking. In: The 2024 ACM Conference on Fairness, Accountability, and Transparency, pp. 1531–1543 (2024)
8. Budach, L., et al.: The effects of data quality on machine learning performance. arXiv preprint arXiv:2207.14529 (2022)
9. Gudivada, V.N., Apon, A., Ding, J.: Data quality considerations for big data and machine learning: going beyond data cleaning and transformations. Int. J. Adv. Softw. **10**(1), 1–20 (2017)
10. Dwivedi, Y.K., et al.: So what if ChatGPT wrote it? Multidisciplinary perspectives on opportunities, challenges and implications of generative conversational AI for research, practice and policy. Int. J. Inf. Manage. **71**, 102642 (2023)

11. Hartmann, J., Schwenzow, J., Witte, M.: The political ideology of conversational AI: converging evidence on ChatGPT's pro-environmental, left-libertarian orientation. arXiv preprint arXiv:2301.01768 (2023)
12. Fujimoto, S., Takemoto, K.: Revisiting the political biases of ChatGPT. Front. Artif. Intell. **6**, 1232003 (2023)
13. Jones, B., Luger, E., Jones, R.: Generative AI & Journalism: A Rapid Risk-Based Review. Edinburgh Research Explorer, University of Edinburgh (2023)
14. Wach, K., et al.: The dark side of generative artificial intelligence: a critical analysis of controversies and risks of ChatGPT. Entrep. Bus. Econ. Rev. **11**(2), 7–30 (2023)
15. Bontcheva, K., et al.: Generative AI and Disinformation: Recent Advances, Challenges, and Opportunities. European Digital Media Observatory (2024)
16. Spitale, G., Biller-Andorno, N., Germani, F.: AI model GPT-3 (dis) informs us better than humans. arXiv preprint arXiv:2301.11924 (2023)
17. Hanley, H.W.A., Durumeric, Z.: Machine-made media: monitoring the mobilization of machine-generated articles on misinformation and mainstream news websites. arXiv preprint arXiv:2305.09820 (2023)
18. Rawte, V., Sheth, A., Das, A.: A survey of hallucination in large foundation models. arXiv preprint arXiv:2309.05922 (2023)
19. Dignum, V.: Responsible artificial intelligence: designing AI for human values. ITU J. ICT Discov. **1**, 1–8 (2017)
20. Johnson, B., Smith, J.: Towards ethical data-driven software: filling the gaps in ethics research & practice. In: 2021 IEEE/ACM 2nd International Workshop on Ethics in Software Engineering Research and Practice (SEthics) (2021)
21. Khan, A.A., et al.: Ethics of AI: a systematic literature review of principles and challenges. In: Proceedings of the 26th International Conference on Evaluation and Assessment in Software Engineering, pp. 383–392 (2022)
22. Stahl, B.C.: Concepts of ethics and their application to AI. In: Artificial Intelligence for a Better Future. SRIG, pp. 19–33. Springer, Cham (2021). https://doi.org/10.1007/978-3-030-69978-9_3
23. Jahan, N., Naveed, S., Zeshan, M., Tahir, M.A.: How to conduct a systematic review: a narrative literature review. Cureus **8**(11), e864 (2016)
24. Baumeister, R.F., Leary, M.R.: Writing narrative literature reviews. Rev. Gen. Psychol. **1**(3), 311–320 (1997)
25. Rother, E.T.: Systematic literature review X narrative review. Acta Paulista de Enfermagem **20**, v–vi (2007)
26. Dierickx, L., Lindén, C.-G., Opdahl, A.L.: Automated fact-checking to support professional practices: systematic literature review and meta-analysis. Int. J. Commun. **17**, 21 (2023)
27. Dierickx, L., Lindén, C., Opdahl, A.: The information disorder level (IDL) index: a human-based metric to assess the factuality of machine-generated content. In: Multidisciplinary International Symposium On Disinformation in Open Online Media, pp. 60–71 (2023)
28. Singer, J.B.: Border patrol: the rise and role of fact-checkers and their challenge to journalists' normative boundaries. Journalism **22**(8), 1929–1946 (2021)
29. Mena, P.: Principles and boundaries of fact-checking: journalists' perceptions. Journal. Pract. **13**(6), 657–672 (2019)
30. Chen, C., Shu, K.: Combating misinformation in the age of LLMs: opportunities and challenges. arXiv preprint arXiv:2311.05656 (2023)

31. Shapiro, I., Brin, C., Bédard-Brûlé, I., Mychajlowycz, K.: Verification as a strategic ritual: how journalists retrospectively describe processes for ensuring accuracy. Journal. Pract. **7**(6), 657–673 (2013)

32. Martin, N., Comm, B. A.: Information verification in the age of digital journalism. In: Special Libraries Association Annual Conference, Vancouver (2014)

33. Hermida, A.: Tweets and truth: journalism as a discipline of collaborative verification. Journal. Pract. **6**(5–6), 659–668 (2012)

34. Graves, L., Amazeen, M.A.: Fact-checking as idea and practice in journalism. In: Oxford Research Encyclopedia of Communication. Oxford University Press, Oxford (2019)

35. Brandtzaeg, P.B., Lüders, M., Spangenberg, J., Rath-Wiggins, L., Følstad, A.: Emerging journalistic verification practices concerning social media. Journal. Pract. **10**(3), 323–342 (2016)

36. Konstantinovskiy, L., Price, O., Babakar, M., Zubiaga, A.: Toward automated fact-checking: developing an annotation schema and benchmark for consistent automated claim detection. Digit. Threats Res. Pract. **2**(2), 1–16 (2021)

37. Vlachos, A., Riedel, S.: Fact checking: task definition and dataset construction. In: Proceedings of the ACL 2014 Workshop on Language Technologies and Computational Social Science, pp. 18–22 (2014)

38. Sheikhi, G., Touileb, S., Khan, S.: Automated claim detection for fact-checking: a case study using Norwegian pre-trained language models. In: Proceedings of the 24th Nordic Conference on Computational Linguistics (NoDaLiDa), pp. 1–9 (2023)

39. Al-Ghamdi, L.M.: Towards adopting AI techniques for monitoring social media activities. Sustain. Eng. Innov. **3**(1), 15–22 (2021)

40. Himma-Kadakas, M., Ojamets, I.: Debunking false information: investigating journalists' fact-checking skills. Digit. Journal. **10**(5), 866–887 (2022)

41. Johnson, P.R.: A case of claims and facts: automated fact-checking the future of journalism's authority. Digit. Journal. **1–24** (2023)

42. Hassan, N., Arslan, F., Li, C., Tremayne, M.: Toward automated fact-checking: detecting check-worthy factual claims by ClaimBuster. In: Proceedings of the 23rd ACM SIGKDD International Conference on Knowledge Discovery and Data Mining, pp. 1803–1812 (2017)

43. Atanasova, P., et al.: Automatic fact-checking using context and discourse information. J. Data Inf. Qual. (JDIQ) **11**(3), 1–27 (2019)

44. Guo, Z., Schlichtkrull, M., Vlachos, A.: A survey on automated fact-checking. Trans. Assoc. Comput. Linguist. **10**, 178–206 (2022)

45. Locholor, S., Kruikemeier, S.: Re-evaluating journalistic routines in a digital age. New Media Soc. **18**(1), 156–171 (2016)

46. Lim, C.: Checking how fact-checkers check. Res. Polit. **5**(3), 2053168018786848 (2018)

47. Steensen, S., Kalsnes, B., Westlund, O.: The limits of live fact-checking: epistemological consequences of introducing a breaking news logic to political fact-checking. New Media Soc., 14614448231151436 (2023)

48. Nakov, P., et l.: Automated fact-checking for assisting human fact-checkers. In: Proceedings of the Thirtieth International Joint Conference on Artificial Intelligence, Montreal, Canada, pp. 4826–4832. IJCAI (2021)

49. Müller, N., Wiik, J.: From gatekeeper to gate-opener: open-source spaces in investigative journalism. Journal. Pract. **17**, 189–208 (2023)

50. Powers, M.: In forms that are familiar and yet-to-be invented. Am. Journal. Discourse Technol. Specific Work. J. Commun. Inq. **36**(1), 24–43 (2012)

51. Olsen, G.R.: Enthusiasm and alienation: how implementing automated journalism affects the work meaningfulness of three newsroom groups. Journal. Pract., 1–17 (2023)
52. Lopez, M.G., Porlezza, C., Cooper, G., Makri, S., MacFarlane, A., Missaoui, S.: A question of design: strategies for embedding AI-driven tools into journalistic work routines. Digit. Journal. **11**(3), 484–503 (2023)
53. Dierickx, L., Lindén, C.G.: Journalism and fact-checking technologies: understanding user needs. Communication+1 **10**(1) (2023)
54. Samuelsen, R.J., Kalsnes, B., Steensen, S.: The relevance of technology to information verification: insights from norwegian journalism during a national election. Journal. Pract. **1–20** (2023)
55. Edwardsson, M.P., Al-Saqaf, W., Nygren, G.: Verification of digital sources in Swedish newsrooms-a technical issue or a question of newsroom culture? Journal. Pract. **17**(8), 1678–1695 (2023)
56. Weikmann, T., Lecheler, S.: Cutting through the hype: understanding the implications of deepfakes for the fact-checking actor-network. Digit. Journal. **1–18** (2023)
57. Reese, S.D.: Exploring the institutional space of journalism. Problemi dell Informazione **48**(1) (2023)
58. Pastor-Galindo, J., Nespoli, P., Mármol, F., Pérez, G.: The not yet exploited goldmine of OSINT: opportunities, open challenges and future trends. IEEE Access. **8**, 10282–10304 (2020)
59. Westlund, O., Larsen, R., Graves, L., Kavtaradze, L., Steensen, S.: Technologies and fact-checking: a sociotechnical mapping. In: Disinformation Studies: Perspectives from An Emerging Field, pp. 193–236. Labcom Communication & Arts, Covilhã, Portugal (2022)
60. Lindén, C.G.: What makes a reporter human? A research agenda for augmented journalism. Questions de communication **37**, 337–351 (2020)
61. Shkliarevsky, G.: The Emperor with No Clothes: Chomsky Against ChatGPT (2023). Available at SSRN 4439662
62. Larssen, U.: "But verifying facts is what we do!": fact-checking and journalistic professional autonomy. In: Democracy and Fake News: Information Manipulation and Post-Truth Politics, pp. 199–213. Routledge, London (2020)
63. Komatsu, T., et l.: AI should embody our values: investigating journalistic values to inform AI technology design. In: Proceedings of the 11th Nordic Conference on Human-Computer Interaction: Shaping Experiences, Shaping Society, pp. 1–13, Association for Computing Machinery, New York (2020)
64. Schapals, A.K., Porlezza, C.: Assistance or resistance? Evaluating the intersection of automated journalism and journalistic role conceptions. Media Commun. **8**(3), 16–26 (2020)
65. Graves, L., Cherubini, F.: The rise of fact-checking sites in Europe. Digital News Project Report (2016)
66. Ward, S.J.A.: Global journalism ethics: widening the conceptual base. Glob. Media J. **1**, 137 (2008)
67. de Haan, Y., van den Berg, E., Goutier, N., Kruikemeier, S., Lecheler, S.: Invisible friend or foe? How journalists use and perceive algorithmic-driven tools in their research process. Digit. Journal. **10**(10), 1775–1793 (2022)
68. Leiser, M.: Bias, journalistic endeavours, and the risks of artificial intelligence. In: Editor, F., Editor, S. (eds.) Artificial Intelligence and the Media, pp. 8–32. Edward Elgar Publishing, Cheltenham (2022)

69. Ferrario, A., Loi, M.: How explainability contributes to trust in AI. In: Proceedings of the 2022 ACM Conference on Fairness, Accountability, and Transparency, pp. 1457–1466. Association for Computing Machinery, New York (2022)

70. Jacovi, A., Marasović, A., Miller, T., Goldberg, Y.: Formalizing trust in artificial intelligence: prerequisites, causes and goals of human trust in AI. In: Proceedings of the 2021 ACM Conference on Fairness, Accountability, and Transparency, pp. 624–635. Association for Computing Machinery, New York (2021)

71. Lim, G., Perrault, S.T.: Explanation Preferences in XAI Fact-Checkers. European Society for Socially Embedded Technologies (EUSSET) (2022)

72. Micallef, N., Armacost, V., Memon, N., and Patil, S.: True or false: studying the work practices of professional fact-checkers. In: Proceedings of the ACM on Human-Computer Interaction, vol. 6, pp. 1–44. Association for Computing Machinery, New York (2022)

73. Nguyen, A.T., Kharosekar, A., Krishnan, S., Tate, E., Wallace, B.C., Lease, M.: Believe it or not: designing a human-AI partnership for mixed-initiative fact-checking. In: Proceedings of the 31st Annual ACM Symposium on User Interface Software and Technology, pp. 189–199. Association for Computing Machinery, New York (2018)

74. Demartini, G., Mizzaro, S., Spina, D.: Human-in-the-loop artificial intelligence for fighting online misinformation: challenges and opportunities. IEEE Data Eng. Bull. **43**(3), 65–74 (2020)

75. Hamed, A. A., Zachara-Szymanska, M., Wu, X.: Safeguarding authenticity for mitigating the harms of generative AI: Issues, research agenda, and policies for detection, fact-checking, and ethical AI. iScience **27**(2), 108782 (2024)

76. Van Witsen, A., Takahashi, B.: How science journalists verify numbers and statistics in news stories: towards a theory. Journal. Pract. **1–20** (2021)

77. Stray, J.: Making artificial intelligence work for investigative journalism. In: Thurman, N., Lewis, S.C., Kunert, J. (eds.) Algorithms, Automation, and News, pp. 97–118. Routledge, London (2021)

78. Montoro-Montarroso, A., et al.: Fighting disinformation with artificial intelligence: fundamentals, advances and challenges. Profesional de la información **32**(3) (2023)

79. Currie, G.M.: Academic integrity and artificial intelligence: is ChatGPT hype, hero or heresy? In: Seminars in Nuclear Medicine, pp. 1–13. Springer, Heidelberg (2023)

80. Ji, Z., et al.: Survey of hallucination in natural language generation. ACM Comput. Surv. **55**(12), 1–38 (2023)

81. Li, Z.: The dark side of chatGPT: legal and ethical challenges from stochastic parrots and hallucination. arXiv preprint arXiv:2304.14347 (2023)

82. Ray, P.P.: ChatGPT: a comprehensive review on background, applications, key challenges, bias, ethics, limitations and future scope. Internet Things Cyber-Phys. Syst. **3**(1), 121–154 (2023)

83. Yu, W.: A survey of knowledge-enhanced text generation. ACM Comput. Surv. **54**(11s), 1–38 (2022)

84. Kreps, S., McCain, R.M., Brundage, M.: All the news that's fit to fabricate: AI-generated text as a tool of media misinformation. J. Exp. Political Sci. **9**(1), 104–117 (2022)

85. Brugger, F., Gehrke, C.: Skilling and deskilling: technological change in classical economic theory and its empirical evidence. Theory Soc. **47**, 663–689 (2018)

86. Polyportis, A., Pahos, N.: Navigating the perils of artificial intelligence: a focused review on ChatGPT and responsible research and innovation. Humanit. Soc. Sci. Commun. **11**(1), 1–10 (2024)
87. LaGrandeur, K.: The consequences of AI hype. AI Ethics, 1–4 (2023)
88. van Dalen, A.: Algorithmic Gatekeeping for Professional Communicators: Power, Trust, and Legitimacy. Taylor & Francis, London (2023)
89. Siau, K., Wang, W.: Building trust in artificial intelligence, machine learning, and robotics. Cutter Bus. Technol. J. **31**(2), 47–53 (2018)
90. Bartneck, C., Lütge, C., Wagner, A., Welsh, S.: Trust and fairness in AI systems. In: An Introduction to Ethics in Robotics and AI. SE, pp. 27–38. Springer, Cham (2021). https://doi.org/10.1007/978-3-030-51110-4_4
91. Opdahl, A.L., et al.: Trustworthy journalism through AI. Data Knowl. Eng. **146**, 102182 (2023)
92. Deuze, M., Beckett, C.: Imagination, algorithms and news: developing AI literacy for journalism. Digit. Journal. **10**(10), 1913–1918 (2022)
93. Lopezosa, C., Codina, L., Pont-Sorribes, C., Vállez, M.: Use of generative artificial intelligence in the training of journalists: challenges, uses and training proposal. Profesional de la información/Inf. Prof. **32**(4) (2023)
94. Becker, K., et al.: Policies in parallel? A comparative study of journalistic AI policies in 52 Global News Organisations. *Oxford University Research Archive*, pp. 1–37 (2023)
95. Weisz, J.D., Muller, M., He, J., Houde, S.: Toward general design principles for generative AI applications. arXiv preprint arXiv:2301.05578 (2023)
96. Tonmoy, S.M., et al.: A comprehensive survey of hallucination mitigation techniques in large language models. arXiv preprint arXiv:2401.01313 (2024)
97. Feldman, P., Foulds, J.R., Pan, S.: Trapping LLM hallucinations using tagged context prompts. arXiv preprint arXiv:2306.06085 (2023)
98. Bsharat, S.M., Myrzakhan, A., Shen, Z.: Principled instructions are all you need for questioning LLaMA-1/2, GPT-3.5/4. arXiv preprint arXiv:2312.16171 (2023)
99. White, J., et al.: A prompt pattern catalog to enhance prompt engineering with chatgpt. arXiv preprint arXiv:2302.11382 (2023)
100. Rai, A.: Explainable AI: from black box to glass box. J. Acad. Mark. Sci. **48**, 137–141 (2020)
101. Weber-Wulff, D., et al.: Testing of detection tools for AI-generated text. Int. J. Educ. Integr. **19**(1), 26 (2023)

Leveraging Large Language Models for Fact-Checking Farsi News Headlines

Shirin Dehghani[1], Mohammadmasiha Zahedivafa[2], Zahra Baghshahi[3], Darya Zare[4], Sara Yari[3], Zeynab Samei[5], Mohammadhadi Aliahmadi[2], Mahdis Abbasi[3], Sara Mirzamojtahedi[1], Sarvenaz Ebrahimi[6], and Meysam Alizadeh[6(✉)]

[1] Allameh Tabataba'i University, Tehran, Iran
[2] Iran University of Science and Technology, Tehran, Iran
[3] University of Tehran, Tehran, Iran
[4] Amirkabir University of Technology, Tehran, Iran
[5] Institute for Research in Fundamental Research, Tehran, Iran
[6] University of Zurich, 8050 Zurich, Switzerland
`alizadeh@ipz.uzh.ch`

Abstract. The proliferation of misinformation demands the development of automated fact-checking systems. Large language models (LLMs), are increasingly being used for academic, legal, and journalistic content writing. This underscores the critical importance of LLMs in distinguishing between factual accuracy and inaccuracy. Hence, understanding the capacities and limitations of LLMs in fact-checking tasks is essential for their usage in information space. While previous research showed the potential of LLMs in fact-checking English news headlines, the extent to which LLMs work well in other languages are mostly unexplored. In this paper, using data from a local fact-checking website, we investigate the performance of close- and open-source LLMs in fact-checking Farsi news headlines. Our results show that in none of the model combinations, the fact-checking accuracy of LLMs exceeds 55%, which is pretty low compared to results reported for English news. While fine-tuning shows promising results for performance gain, and should be explored further in future research, our results underscore the weakness of LLMs in low-resource languages such as Farsi, even when fine-tuned.

Keywords: Fact-checking · LLM · ChatGPT · Misinformation · Content Moderation · Farsi News

1 Introduction

There are widespread concerns about the potential adverse impact of Large Language Models (LLMs) and AI tools like ChatGPT and Midjourney on online information ecosystem health. ChatGPT can be weaponized to generate false narratives, such as detailed news articles, while Midjourney and Dall-E can complement it by creating realistic images [16]. There is a particular worry that bad actors, including anti-vaccine communities [20], state-sponsored information operations [3], and political disinformation campaigners [29], will leverage

M. Preuss et al. (Eds.): MISDOOM 2024, LNCS 15175, pp. 16–31, 2024.
https://doi.org/10.1007/978-3-031-71210-4_2

AI and LLM as a force multiplier to propagate harmful false narratives globally. At the same time, ChatGPT is capable of generating text at a pace unmatched by any human and provides an endless amount of nearly cost-free viewpoints, potentially overshadowing genuine human input [12].

Fact-checking has become a vital tool to reduce the spread of misinformation online, shown to potentially reduce an individual's belief in false news and rumors [21]. While verifying a claim is a core task of all journalists, a variety of dedicated fact-checking websites have formed to correct misconceptions, rumors, and fake news online. Examples include 'Politifact' and 'Snopes' in USA, 'FullFact' in UK, and 'Corrective' in Germany.

The potential of LLMs to outpace human contributions and exacerbate online misinformation has implications for existing fact-checking efforts. Interestingly, although LLMs can exacerbate this problem, it can also be leveraged to automatically categorize or fact-check harmful or suspicious statements [12]. This doesn't mean that LLMs are expected, or even yet able, to replace human and expert fact-checkers, as fact-checking is not just about labeling the headlines and requires detailed presentation of facts, which sometime requires purely human activities such as calling an expert on her phone or contacting the office of a politician [10]. Instead, it suggests that it can serve as an extra resource for identifying potential misinformation at scale.

Recent research has explored the potential of using large artificial intelligence language models as a tool for fact-checking [6, 12, 22]. However, significant challenges remain when employing large language models (LLMs) to assess the veracity of a statement. One primary issue is that of low-resource languages. While GPT-4 and LlaMa2 (70b) have shown a significant improvement in cross-lingual comprehension and translation [1, 25], the extent to which they perform well on low-resource languages such as Farsi is mostly unexplored. This is primarily due to the limited amount of pretraining data available in non-English languages [25].

In this study, we evaluate LLMs performance at classifying verified Farsi statements by relying on a database collected from the popular Iranian fact-check website Factyar. The database contains 676 statements from 2021 up to including 2024 that have been fact-checked by experts into one of five categories: true, half true, misleading, half false, and false. Using two different prompts instructing to categorize each of these 676 statements into one of the five categories as defined by Factyar (Factyar prompt) or as a 3-class classification into either true, false, or no verdict, we submitted this task to ChatGPT (GPT-3.5 and GPT-4) and LlaMa (LlaMa2 (70b) and LlaMa2-chat (70b)) as a zero-shot classification. We explore the 3-class prompt for two reasons: (1) low frequency of half-true, half-falses, and misleading labels in the held-out test set; and (2) to extend the generalizability of LLMs performance to other fact-checking instances which may rely on other labeling systems. A binary true/false plus 'no verdict' system can be used across different languages, cultures, and political systems, as the labels are universally understood [12].

2   Previous Work

Since 2010s, a wide array of research have embarked on the journey of automated fact-checking employing diverse methodologies. Several shared tasks
have been introduced, enabling researchers to address identical challenges or
datasets within a predefined framework for outcome evaluation. For instance,
the RUMOUREVAL announced a compilation of "questionable posts along with
subsequent discussions on social media, annotated for both stance and truthfulness" [11]. Later, CLEF CHECKTHAT! initiated three distinct tasks, each
designed to address specific segments within the fact-checking process [18]. The
first task asked predictions on which Twitter posts, particularly those related to
COVID-19 and political matters across six languages, worth fact-checking [17].
The second task sought to identify claims that had already been fact-checked
[19]. The final task, formulated as a multi-class classification challenge, concentrated on assessing the authenticity of news articles in both German and
English [14]. Moreover, the Fact Extraction and VERification (FEVER) shared
task impelled participants to categorize factoid claims crafted by humans as
either SUPPORTED or REFUTED based on evidence sourced from Wikipedia
[24]. In general, these challenges and the proposed resolutions deconstruct the
fact-checking process into a series of distinct stages, acknowledging that detection, contextualization, and verification each necessitate tailored approaches and
techniques [7].

After the introduction of ChatGPT in 2023, researchers attention shifted
from BERT and RoBERTa to ChatGPT. In their seminal work, Hoes et al. [12]
tested GPT-3.5's claim verification performance on a dataset of PolitiFact statements without adding any context. The results showed that GPT-3.5 performs
well on the dataset and argue that it shows the potential of leveraging GPT-
3.5 and other LLMs for enhancing the efficiency and expediency of the fact-
checking process. Another work, compared GPT-3 with different BERT models
for evaluating the check-worthiness of short texts in English [23]. They find that
fine-tuned BERT models perform on par to GPT-3. Choi and Ferrara [6] used
fact-checks to construct a synthetic dataset of contradicting, supporting or neutral claims and introduced FACT-GPT. They create the synthetic data using
GPT-4 and predict the entailment using a smaller fine-tuned LLM. The found
that fine-tuned LLMs rival the performance of larger pre-trained LLMs in claim
matching tasks, aligning closely with human annotations. Similarly, Caramancion [5] compared the performance of Bard (now Gemini), BingAI, GPT-3.5,
and GPT-4 on discerning the truthfulness of 100 fact-checked news items. The
authors find that all LLMs achieve performances of around 64–71% accuracy,
with GPT 4 receiving the highest score among all LLMs.

One limitation of the above research is lack of access to contextual data.
That is, the LLMs used in previous research were not able to access external data on the statement through performing web search. In a recent study,
Quelle and Bovet [22] relaxed this limitation and test the ability of GPT-3.5
& 4 to perform fact-checking using a specialized dataset. Their results show
that (1) incorporating contextual information (through web search) significantly

improves fact-checking accuracy; (2) GPT-4 significantly outperforms GPT-3.5 at fact-checking claims; and (3) fact-checking performance varies substantially across languages, with non-English claims see a large boost when translated to English before being fed to LLMs. Although these results are promising, they have two major limitations. First, using GPT-4 is costly, specially for countries with low currency valuation. It is importatn to note that most fact-checking organization are non-profit and non-governmental and mostly rely on donations, and hence, may not afford GPT-4 at a long run. Second, the extend to which their results are generalizable for a low-resource language such as Farsi is questionable.

In this paper, we extend the Quelle and Bovet [22]'s work in two ways: (1) we examine the perfomance of GPT-3.5 and GPT-4 on Farsi statements; and (2) we explore the ability of the open-source (and free to use) LlaMa2 model to perform fact-checking on Farsi statements. Following [22], we compare the results of these LLM with and without access to external data through web search.

3   Data and Methods

3.1   Data

We relied on a database collected from a popular Iranian fact-checking website Factyar (www.factyar.com). The dataset contains 676 statements from 21 June 2021 up to 15 March 2024 that are fact-checked by experts into one of the following six categories: true, half true, misleading, half false, and false. In the methods section, Factyar's experts mention that since they cannot feasibly check all claims, they have selected those news headlines that met these criteria: newsworthy, rooted in facts and are thus verifiable, and viral on social media. In our analysis, we rely on the full dataset. Table 1 shows the frequency of news headlines in each of the above six categories.

Table 1. Frequencies of fact-check data across six classes.

Label	Description	Freq.
True	Accurate and there's nothing significant missing	320
False	Statement is not accurate	166
Half True	Partially accurate but lacks details or takes things out of context	85
Half False	Partially inaccurate but contains some accurate facts	67
Misleading	Contains truth but ignores facts that gives a different impression	38
Total		676

We take the top 200 oldest statements as a training set and use the remaining 476 statements as a held-out test set. The held-out test set includes 225 true, 108 false, 64 half true, 47 half false, and 32 misleading statements. The earliest statement in the test set is for 16/08/2021. The 200 training data includes 95 true, 58 false, 21 half true, 20 half false, and 6 misleading statements.

3.2   LLM Annotation Tasks

We explore the ability of GPT and LlaMa models in fact-checking Farsi statements along three dimensions: (1) number of classes; (2) access to external data; and (3) fine-tuning. First, following [12], in addition to the five classes mentioned above, we also consider a binary true/false classification with 'no verdict' being the third class. Second, following [22], we compare the performance of LLMs with and without access to external contextual data through web search. Finally, following [2] that showed fine-tuned open-source LLMs perform on par with GPT-3.5 in text annotation, we use the 200 training data points to fine-tune LlaMa2 (70b) and GPT-3.5 (we still have not access to GPT-4 fine-tuning API) with fine-tuning size of 100. For all prompts, since this is a text classification task, we set the temperature parameter to 0.1. This approach emphasizes outputs with the highest probability, making them more deterministic and suitable for a scientific paper.

3.3   Prompt Optimization

To enhance the performance of large language models, we employed a prompt-based optimization method OPRO. This approach provides a straightforward, effective, and efficient means of utilizing large language models as optimizers [28]. During each step of the optimization process, the large language model (LLM) generates potential solutions by referencing both the problem description and the solutions previously assessed in the meta-prompt. These new solutions are then evaluated and incorporated into the meta-prompt to guide further optimization. The process concludes either when the LLM fails to generate superior solutions with improved optimization scores, or when a predefined maximum number of steps is reached. Initially, we delineate the essential attributes of LLMs for effective optimization, followed by an exposition of the principal design decisions informed by these attributes.

3.4   Model Selection and Setting

To evaluate the fact-checking performance and cost efficiency of various large language models (LLMs), we selected two close-source and two open-source distinct LLMs. Our selection of close-source model is OPENAI's GPT (GPT-4 and GPT-3.5 ('gpt-3.5-turbo' version)), a proprietary, closed-source LLM. For open-source LLM evaluation, we chose Meta's LLaMA2 in two configurations: LLaMA2 (70b) and LlaMa2-chat (70b). We used HuggingChat's implementation of LlaMa2-chat for zero-shot classification.

3.5   LLM Fine-Tuning

Pretraining Large Language Models (LLMs) on extensive corpora enables them to perform competently across a wide range of tasks with minimal examples, often achieving results that rival those of fine-tuned transformer models [4].

Specifically, in contexts where the LLM has not been sufficiently trained on task-relevant data, supervised fine-tuning can offer advantages. This involves supplementing the model with an additional dataset of labeled task-specific examples and selectively updating a subset of its weight parameters [26]. However, while effective, fine-tuning such extensive models, particularly those with tens to hundreds of billions of parameters, can be computationally intensive, often requiring large-scale GPU clusters. However, recent advancements have made it feasible to fine-tune these models on single-GPU systems by employing techniques such as 4-bit or 8-bit quantization and adding lower-rank adapter layers to the original architecture [8].

In GPT-3.5, the fine-tuning process bridges the generalized learning acquired from pre-training and the specialized learning required for domain-specific Tasks. OpenAI's GPT-3.5 architecture permits fine-tuning via its specialized Application Programming Interface (API), encompassing a multi-step workflow. Initially, the procedure necessitates the preparation of domain-specific datasets, generally constituting labeled instances. The transformation of this data involves segregating the input into three distinct components as mandated by the API. The first segment comprises the system prompt, articulating the overarching task instruction (e.g., Definition, Steps, Examples, etc.). Subsequently, the second segment encapsulates the user prompt, laden with domain-specific data and the instruction that requires labeling. The final segment incorporates the assistant prompt, directly indicating the target labels.

Acting as a facilitative mechanism, the API enables users to delineate the training configuration, offering the liberty to customize hyperparameters, such as the number of epochs. Once the configuration is established and data uploaded, the API initiates the fine-tuning process. The model parameters are then updated iteratively to minimize the loss on the fine-tuning dataset. However, the inner workings of the fine-tuning process remain somewhat opaque, limiting interpretability and potential improvements. Post-fine-tuning, the model is evaluated on a held-out dataset to ascertain its performance on the target task. The fine-tuned model can then be deployed for the desired application.

We employed a combination of techniques to achieve efficient adaptation for fine-tuning the Open Source Models. Low-Rank Adaptation (LoRA) significantly reduces the number of trainable parameters by introducing low-rank matrices into each layer that capture task-specific adjustments [13]. Additionally, 4-bit quantization compresses the pre-trained model weights from 32-bit floating-point numbers to a more memory-efficient 4-bit representation, as described in [9]. This combination allows us to perform supervised fine-tuning on large models such as 'LlaMa2 (70b)' [15] with better efficiency and potentially faster training times. We used adapter layers on the Query and Value attention blocks in all cases. As the training sets for each task are small and all are text classification tasks, we chose $r = 16$ and $\alpha = 32$ as hyperparameters for the adapter layers added. A lower rank was chosen to avoid overfitting to the training set, while the α was selected to produce a scaling of 2 and give more weight to the output of the adaptive layers and force the LLMs to follow the format used in the training set examples. As for the hyperparameters during training, we chose the default parameters of the Seq2SeqTrainer and SFTTrainer from huggingface [27].

For LLaMA2, we needed three 80GB A100 GPUs for the 70b model. To optimize training efficiency, the input text for both models (LLaMA2 & LLaMA2-chat) was left-truncated at a maximum of 4096 tokens. This combination of prompt design, targeted allocation of computational resources, and adherence to established prompting strategies facilitated effective fine-tuning of the LLaMA models. We trained all LLMs for three epochs with a batch size of four. To further improve efficiency, we implemented a technique called gradient accumulation, where the model weights were only updated after accumulating gradients from every second batch.

3.6 Evaluation Metrics

We computed average accuracy (i.e. percentage of correct predictions), that is, the number of correctly classified instances over the total number of cases to be classified, using trained human annotations as our gold standard and considering only texts that both annotators agreed upon.

4 Results

4.1 Optimised Prompt

According to Sect. 3.3, we use the OPRO method to improve our prompts based on a main prompt. We also use two large language models (LLMs) for this improvement: one as an optimizer and the other as a scorer. For problems involving both three categories and five categories, we usually use the same model for both optimizing and scoring. However, we made an exception for the LLaMA2 (70b) model. This model did not work well in creating prompts from the main prompt, so we used the LLaMA2-chat (70b) model instead for optimizing. We set the temperature to 1 for all optimizers and to 0.1 for all scorers. Tables 2 and 3 (in appendix) shows the optimized prompt for both 3 classes and 5 classes problems. For translating the claims to English, we used google translate API[1].

4.2 Zero-Shot LLMs

In this analysis, we compare four large language models using optimized prompts for zero-shot classification in both 3 class and 5 class problems. We use zero-shot classification as a baseline for each model, which involves providing the claims directly to the optimized prompt without accessing external data or translation to English. To enhance this method, we also evaluate the performance of the LLMs when the claims are translated to English and then fed to the optimized prompt. Figure 1 displays the accuracy of zero-shot classification for both 3 and 5 class problems. In the 3 class problem, all models with translation to English

---

[1] https://pypi.org/project/googletrans/.

outperform the baseline (where we fed the claim in Farsi language to the prompt). The only exception is GPT-3.5, which slightly underperforms when working with an English translated claim. For the five-class problem, with the exception of LLaMA2-chat (70b), all models in the translation format perform better than the baseline model.

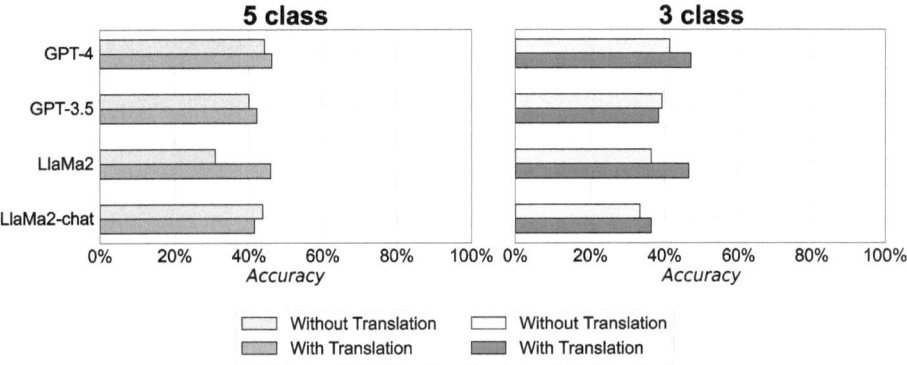

Fig. 1. Accuracy of zero-shot LLMs for classifying claims that fact-checkers have already rated. The 5 class panel (left) shows the results with respect to the original lables used by the Iranian fact-checking website. The 3 class panel (right) shows the results when LLMs are prompted to a simpler problem (true, false, no verdict). All prompts have been optimized using the OPRO method.

4.3 LLMs with Access to External Data

One of the recent developments in LLMs is enabling them to access external data. In this section, we evaluate the performance of GPT-4, GPT-3.5, and LLaMA2-chat (70b) models using optimized prompts and with access to external data (Google search). For GPT-4, we enabled it to access external data through a web user-interface with the instruction to "Browse the internet and show the references, and don't use Persian(Farsi) fact-checking references" at the end of the initial prompt. For LLaMA2-chat (70b) and GPT-3.5, we used a combination of iterative searching and agent-based reasoning to improve automated claim verification. We enabled these models to utilize the Google Search engine to collect relevant information [22]. To prevent direct access to fact-checkers websites, we filtered out search results from domains listed in the dataset. The models received data from the Google Search Engine API, which included summaries of search results, each containing the website's title, a link, and a snippet of relevant content, simulating a typical user experience on Google.

Figure 2 illustrates the accuracy of GPT-4, GPT-3.5, and LLaMA2-chat (70b) in classifying Farsi claims that have already been rated by fact-checkers. The baseline is zero-shot with prompt optimization and without access to Google search. We show the results for both 3 and 5 class problems. Surprisingly, for the 5 class problem (i.e. the orginal rating system of the Iranian fact-ckecking website), enabling the LLMs to access Google search results decreased the perfromance of the LLM in claim fact-checking (left panel in Fig. 2. However, for the 3-class problem (i.e. true, false, or no verdict), the accuracy of GPT-4 increased from 41.4% to 42.0%, for LLaMA2-chat from 33.3% to 35.3%, while the accuracy of GPT-3.5 slightly decreased from 39.3% to 39.0%.

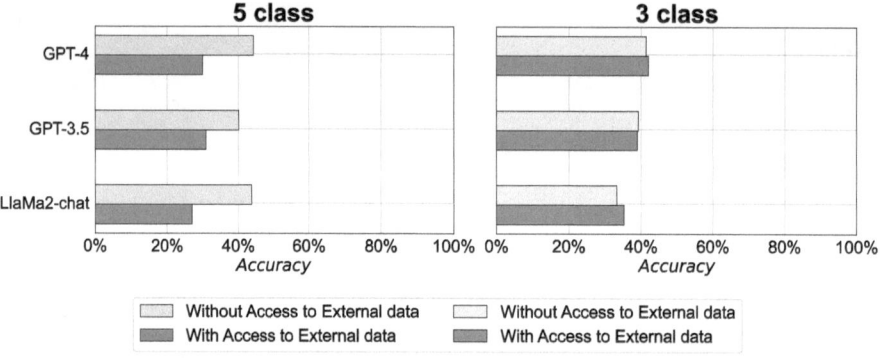

Fig. 2. Accuracy of zero-shot LLMs with access to external data for classifying claims that fact-checkers have already rated.

4.4   Fine-Tuning LLMs

We selected GPT-3.5, LLaMa2 (70b), and LLaMa2-chat (70b) because they are capable of being fine-tuned. We compared the accuracy of these three LLMs when fine-tuned with 100 fact-checked claims with those of zero-shot baselines for both 3 and 5 classification problems. Acting as a facilitative mechanism, their APIs enables users to delineate the training configuration, offering the liberty to customize hyperparameters, such as the number of epochs. Once the configuration is established and data uploaded, the API initiates the fine-tuning process. The model parameters are then updated iteratively to minimize the loss on the fine-tuning dataset. However, the inner workings of the fine-tuning process remain somewhat opaque, limiting interpretability and potential improvements. Post-fine-tuning, the model is evaluated on a held-out dataset to ascertain its performance on the target task. The fine-tuned model can then be deployed for the desired application.

Figure 3 displays our fine-tuning results for fact-checking of Farsi claims in the original five-rating classification of the Iranian fact-checking website (i.e. Factyar) across four different problem categories. Panel A in Fig. 3 shows how much performance gain we obtained by fine-tuning compared to the zero-shot reasoning (no optimized prompt, no access to external data, and no translation of claims to English) reported in Sect. 4.2. The results show that, across all three considered LLMs, fine-tuning with 100 instances of fact-checked claims improves the accuracy of LLMs, with fine-tuned GPT-3.5 achieving the highest performance.

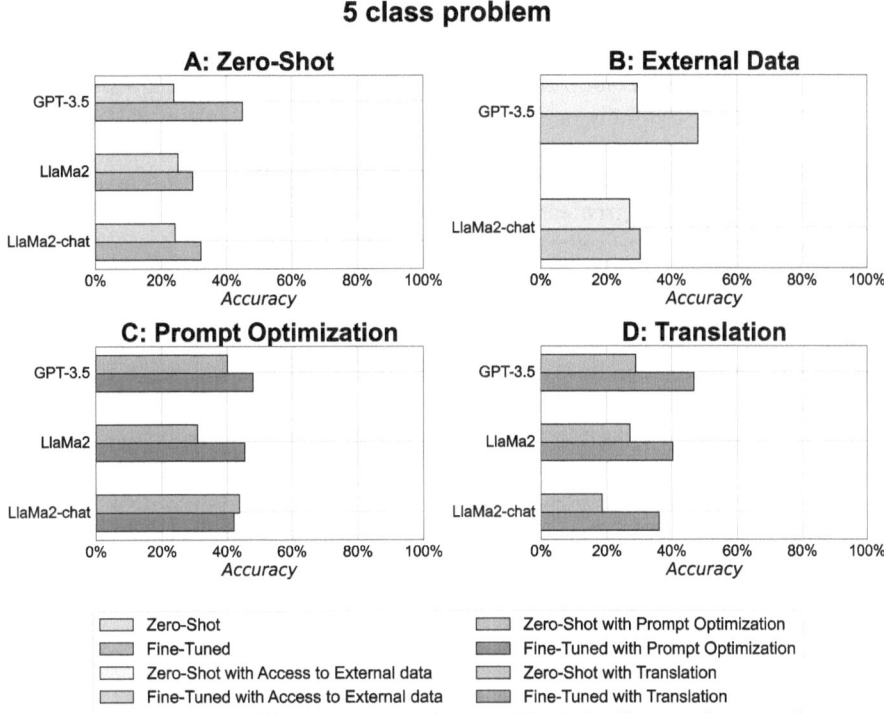

Fig. 3. Comparing Accuracy of Zero-Shot and Fine-Tuning for **5 class** problem.

Panel B in Fig. 3 compares the accuracy of fine-tuned GPT-3.5 and LlaMa2-chat with the zero-shot results where both have access to external data. In both scenarios, no optimized prompt or translation of claims to English has been used.

The results exhibit a significant performance improvement for fine-tuned models, specially for GPT-3.5. More particularly, we see a 18.8% point increase in the accuracy of GPT-3.5 and 3.2% point increase in the accuracy of the LlaMa2-chat (70b) models.

Panel C in Fig. 3 shows how much performance gain we obtained by fine-tuning compared to the zero-shot reasoning with optimized prompt (no access to external data and no translation of claims to English). The results show that, with the exception of LlaMa2-chat (70b), the other two LLMs significantly benefited from fine-tuning. While the best performing model in terms of accuracy is fine-tuned GPT-3.5, the LlaMa2 (70b) benefited the most from fine-tuning by gaining 14.6% point performance.

Finally, panel D in Fig. 3 compares the accuracy of fine-tuned LLM with corresponding zero-shot LLMs' results when in both the claims have been translated to English. In both cases, no prompt optimization or access to external data were allowed. Across all three LLMs, we can see that fine-tuning with 100 instances of fact-checked claims has considerably increased the accuracy of models in fact-checking Farsi claims. Similar to previous panels of Fig. 3, fine-tuned GPT-3.5 achieved the best performance, with LlaMa2 (70b) and LlaMa2-chat (70b) in the second and third positions. An interesting observation is across all three LLMs, we see the greatest performance gains for 'translation to English' scenario compared to the other three scenarios described in Fig. 3.

Figure 4 displays our fine-tuning results for fact-checking of Farsi claims in the three classification ratings (i.e. true, false, and no verdict) across four different problem categories. Overall, the results are similar to those of the 5 class reasoning explained in Fig. 3. Four important observation stand out in Fig. 4: (1) fine-tuned GPT-3.5 achieves the best accuracy across all four problem categories (i.e. zer-shot, access to external data, prompt optimization, and translation to English; (2) the largest performance gain from fine-tuning happens when the claims are translated to English; (3) both versions of the LlaMa2 (70b), which are open-source and free to use, exhibit comparable accuracy with that of GPT-3.5; (4) across all categories, even when LLMs are fine-tuned and fed with English translation of claims, their accuracy are below 50%, which highlights the underperformance of LLMs in low-resource languages.

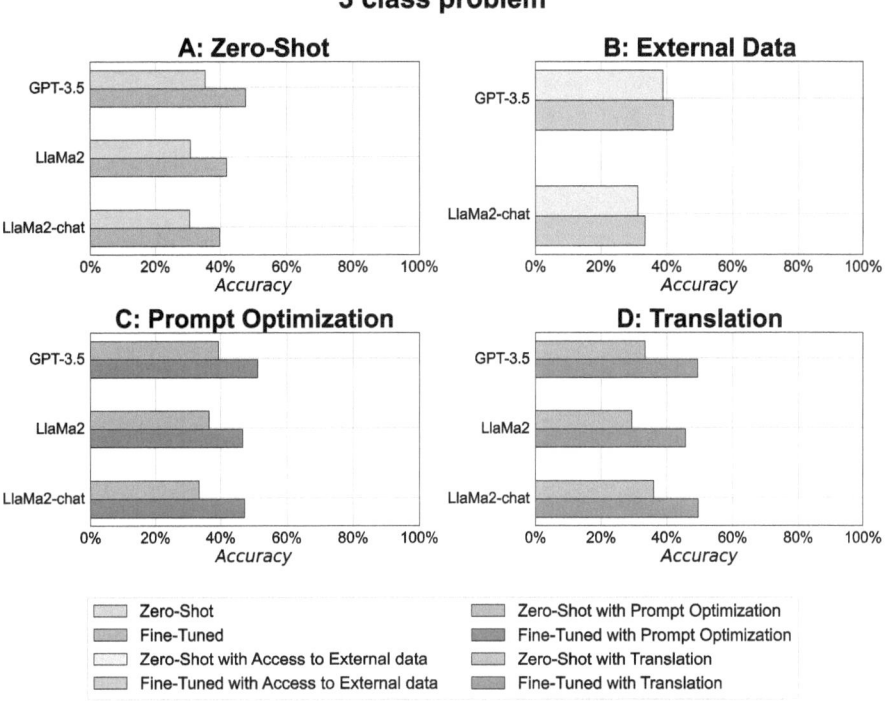

Fig. 4. Comparing Accuracy of Zero-Shot and Fine-Tuning for **3 class** problem.

5   Conclusion

In this study, we investigate the potential of using GPT and LlaMa2 LLMs for fact-checking Farsi (Persian) claims. We explored several previously proven methods of improving the performance of LLMs including fine-tuning, prompt optimization, access to external data (i.e. allow LLMs to search Google), and translation to English. The most important result of this study is that in none of the model combinations, the fact-checking accuracy of LLMs exceeds 55%, which is pretty low compared to results reported for English news. For example, in fact-checking of PolitiFact's claims, ChatGPT's accuracy varied between 64% to 82% depending on the topic and classification task [12]. While fine-tuning shows promising results for performance gain, and should be explored further in future research, our results underscore the weakness of LLMs in low-resource languages such as Farsi, even when fine-tuned.

Acknowledgments. We thank Factyar team (an Iranian NGO fact-checking website) for providing easy acess to their fact-checked data.

Disclosure of Interests. The authors declare no conflict of interest.

A Appendix

Table 2. Optimized prompt for 3-class problem in both Farsi and translated claims. 'Farsi' refers to training samples (claims) that are in the Farsi language, while 'translated' indicates that our training samples (claims) have been translated into English.

LLM	Optimized Prompt	Claim Language
GPT-4	As a professional fact-checker, categorize the following statement by simply selecting one of these labels: TRUE (fully accurate, no significant omissions), FALSE (inaccurate, invalid) or MISLEADING (contains truth but omits important facts that alter the overall impression, or cannot be classified as true or false). Remember, no explanations are needed, just label the statement	Farsi
	As a credible evaluator, your role is to assess each statement's truthfulness and categorize it into one of the three given categories: - TRUE: This implies the statement is wholly accurate without any pertinent detail omitted. - FALSE: This suggests the statement is not valid and is completely untrue. - MISLEADING: This label is for a statement which includes elements of truth but excludes crucial facts that alter the overall perception of the statement. If the statement can't be classified as TRUE or FALSE clearly, it will fall under this category. Without adding additional explanations, simply assign one of the labels: TRUE, FALSE or MISLEADING, to each statement	Translated
GPT-3.5	Determine the credibility of a statement based on its accuracy and inclusion of significant facts. Choose one label from TRUE, FALSE, and MISLEADING without providing further explanation	Farsi
	Evaluate the statement and determine if it is entirely accurate and without significant missing information (TRUE), if it lacks validity and is not accurate (FALSE), or if it contains some truth but ignores important facts or cannot be clearly categorized as TRUE or FALSE (MISLEADING)	Translated
LlaMa2-chat	Act as an expert fact-checker and provide a rating (TRUE, FALSE, or MISLEADING) for each statement based on your thorough analysis of its accuracy and completeness, considering multiple credible sources and context where necessary	Farsi
	As an expert fact-checker, carefully evaluate the statement and select one of the following labels: TRUE if the statement is entirely accurate and supported by verifiable evidence, FALSE if the statement is inaccurate or lacks credible sources, or MISLEADING if the statement contains some truth but omits or distorts important context, or if it is ambiguous and open to multiple interpretations	Translated
LlaMa2	Act as a reliable fact-checking assistant and classify the provided statement as either TRUE (completely accurate), FALSE (not accurate at all), or MISLEADING (partially true, misrepresented, or lacking proper context). Ensure your judgment is fair, well-informed, and based on verifiable evidence	Farsi
	Read the statement carefully and label it as TRUE if it is entirely accurate, FALSE if it is not accurate, or MISLEADING if it contains truth but ignores facts that give a different impression	Translated

Table 3. Optimized prompt for 5-class problem in both Farsi and translated claims. 'Farsi' refers to training samples (claims) that are in the Farsi language, while 'translated' indicates that our training samples (claims) have been translated into English.

LLM	Optimized Prompt	Claim Language
GPT-4	Analyze the statement without bias, applying factual evaluation, and configure it into one of these categorical labels: - TRUE: The entire statement is entirely accurate and does not miss anything. - HALF-TRUE: Parts of the statement are accurate but may lack some critical details or may contain a degree of misrepresentation. - MISLEADING: While parts of the statement are accurate, other parts contain inaccuracies or context distortion. - HALF-FALSE: The statement diverges noticeably from the truth yet contains some correct elements. - FALSE: The entire statement contains no valid or truthful elements. Please offer your conclusion by stating solely the appropriate label, without any additional explanation. This task encourages critical thinking, fact-checking, and unbiased interpretation	Farsi
	Evaluate the following statement and convey its level of truthfulness by choosing from the following labels: - TRUE: If the statement is completely correct and all facts presented are accurate. - HALF-TRUE: If the statement has elements of truth but also contains inaccuracies or misses key context. - MISLEADING: If the statement is partially true, but also contains false or misleading information. - HALF-FALSE: If the statement contains a balance of correct and incorrect information, or the correct information is presented in a manipulative or misleading context. - FALSE: If the statement is entirely incorrect, with no factual accuracy. Concisely name one of these labels that best suits the statement, without the need for additional explanation	Translated
GPT-3.5	Identify the level of truthfulness in the statement and provide a corresponding label: -TRUE: The statement is entirely correct and does not have any missing information. -HALF-TRUE: The statement is partially correct, but it has overlooked important details or narrated the issue outside the main context. -MISLEADING: A part of the statement is correct, but another part of it is incorrect and has overlooked the context of the matter. -HALF-FALSE: The statement has overlooked some important truths, but some of its details are correct. -FALSE: The statement is completely incorrect and lacks validity	Farsi
	Provide an expert fact-check for each statement and avoid negation, using the following labels: TRUE- completely correct; HALF-TRUE- partially correct but missing important details; MISLEADING- partially correct but overlooks context; HALF-FALSE- overlooks important truths; FALSE- completely incorrect	Tranlated
LlaMa2-chat	As an expert fact-checker, carefully evaluate the statement's accuracy, context, and relevance. Classify the statement into one of the following labels: -TRUE: The statement is entirely correct, accurate, and complete, with no missing or misleading information. -HALF-TRUE: The statement is partially correct, but lacks important details, context, or clarity, making it incomplete or open to misinterpretation. -MISLEADING: The statement contains a mix of accurate and inaccurate information, or presents information in a way that is likely to deceive or mislead. -HALF-FALSE: The statement contains some accurate information, but also significant inaccuracies, omissions, or distortions that alter its overall meaning. -FALSE: The statement is entirely incorrect, inaccurate, or fabricated, with no basis in fact or evidence. When evaluating the statement, consider the source, evidence, and logical coherence. Be cautious of biases, ambiguities, and emotional appeals. Provide a clear and concise justification for your classification	Farsi
	As an expert fact-checker, carefully evaluate the statement and classify it into one of the following labels: TRUE (entirely correct with no missing information), HALF-TRUE (partially correct but lacks important details or context), MISLEADING (mix of correct and incorrect information, often with omitted context), HALF-FALSE (incorrect with some correct details), or FALSE (completely incorrect with no validity). Consider the statement's accuracy, completeness, and potential biases, and choose the label that best reflects its reliability	Translated
LlaMa2	As an expert fact-checker, carefully evaluate the statement's accuracy, completeness, and context. Classify the statement into one of the following labels: -TRUE: The statement is entirely correct, comprehensive, and accurately represents the facts. -HALF-TRUE: The statement is partially correct, but lacks important details, context, or clarity. -MISLEADING: The statement contains a mix of accurate and inaccurate information, or presents information in a way that is deceptive or misleading. -HALF-FALSE: The statement contains some accurate information, but also significant inaccuracies or omissions. -FALSE: The statement is entirely incorrect, lacks any basis in fact, or is a deliberate fabrication. When evaluating the statement, consider the following factors: the credibility of the source, the presence of evidence or references, the clarity and coherence of the language, and the potential for bias or manipulation. Approach each statement with a critical and nuanced mindset, and strive to provide an accurate and informative label	Farsi

continued

Table 3. continued

LLM	Optimized Prompt	Claim Language
	Act as an expert fact-checker and assign one of the following labels to a statement based on its accuracy and context: TRUE if the statement is entirely correct, HALF-TRUE if it is partially correct but lacks important details or context, MISLEADING if it contains a mix of correct and incorrect information, HALF-FALSE if it is mostly incorrect but contains some truth, and FALSE if it is entirely incorrect. Consider the statement's wording, evidence, and potential biases when making your assessment	Translated

References

1. Achiam, J., et al.: GPT-4 technical report. arXiv preprint arXiv:2303.08774 (2023)
2. Alizadeh, M., et al.: Open-source large language models outperform crowd workers and approach ChatGPT in text-annotation tasks. arXiv preprint arXiv:2307.02179 (2023)
3. Alizadeh, M., Shapiro, J.N., Buntain, C., Tucker, J.A.: Content-based features predict social media influence operations. Sci. Adv. **6**(30), eabb5824 (2020)
4. Brown, T., et al.: Language models are few-shot learners. In: Advances in Neural Information Processing Systems, vol. 33, pp. 1877–1901 (2020)
5. Caramancion, K.M.: News verifiers showdown: a comparative performance evaluation of ChatGPT 3.5, ChatGPT 4.0, Bing AI, and bard in news fact-checking. arXiv preprint arXiv:2306.17176 (2023)
6. Choi, E.C., Ferrara, E.: Automated claim matching with large language models: empowering fact-checkers in the fight against misinformation. arXiv preprint arXiv:2310.09223 (2023)
7. Das, A., Liu, H., Kovatchev, V., Lease, M.: The state of human-centered NLP technology for fact-checking. Inf. Process. Manag. **60**(2), 103219 (2023)
8. Dettmers, T., Pagnoni, A., Holtzman, A., Zettlemoyer, L.: QloRA: efficient fine-tuning of quantized LLMs (2023)
9. Dettmers, T., Pagnoni, A., Holtzman, A., Zettlemoyer, L.: QLoRA: efficient fine-tuning of quantized LLMs. In: Advances in Neural Information Processing Systems, vol. 36 (2024)
10. DeVerna, M.R., Yan, H.Y., Yang, K.C., Menczer, F.: Artificial intelligence is ineffective and potentially harmful for fact checking. arXiv preprint arXiv:2308.10800 (2023)
11. Gorrell, G., Bontcheva, K., Derczynski, L., Kochkina, E., Liakata, M., Zubiaga, A.: RumourEval 2019: determining rumour veracity and support for rumours arXiv preprint arXiv:1809.06683 (2018)
12. Hoes, E., Altay, S., Bermeo, J.: Leveraging ChatGPT for efficient fact-checking (2023)
13. Hu, E.J., et al.: LoRA: low-rank adaptation of large language models. arXiv preprint arXiv:2106.09685 (2021)
14. Köhler, J., et al.: Overview of the CLEF-2022 CheckThat! Lab: task 3 on fake news detection. In: CLEF (Working Notes), pp. 404–421 (2022)
15. Köpf, A., et al.: OpenAssistant conversations – democratizing large language model alignment (2023)
16. Menczer, F., Crandall, D., Ahn, Y.Y., Kapadia, A.: Addressing the harms of AI-generated inauthentic content. Nat. Mach. Intell. **5**(7), 679–680 (2023)

17. Nakov, P., et al.: Overview of the CLEF-2022 CheckThat! Lab task 1 on identifying relevant claims in tweets. In: 2022 Conference and Labs of the Evaluation Forum, CLEF 2022, pp. 368–392. CEUR Workshop Proceedings (CEUR-WS. org) (2022)
18. Nakov, P., et al.: Overview of the CLEF–2022 CheckThat! Lab on fighting the covid-19 infodemic and fake news detection. In: Barrón-Cedeño, A., et al. (eds.) CLEF 2022. LNCS, vol. 13390, pp. 495–520. Springer, Cham (2022). https://doi.org/10.1007/978-3-031-13643-6_29
19. Nakov, P., Da San Martino, G., Alam, F., Shaar, S., Mubarak, H., Babulkov, N.: Overview of the CLEF-2022 CheckThat! Lab task 2 on detecting previously fact-checked claims (2022)
20. Pierri, F., DeVerna, M.R., Yang, K.C., Axelrod, D., Bryden, J., Menczer, F.: One year of covid-19 vaccine misinformation on twitter: longitudinal study (preprint) (2022)
21. Porter, E., Wood, T.J.: The global effectiveness of fact-checking: Evidence from simultaneous experiments in Argentina, Nigeria, South Africa, and the United Kingdom. Proc. Natl. Acad. Sci. **118**(37), e2104235118 (2021)
22. Quelle, D., Bovet, A.: The perils and promises of fact-checking with large language models. Front. Artif. Intell. **7**, 1341697 (2024)
23. Sawiński, M., et al.: OpenFact at CheckThat! 2023: head-to-head GPT vs. BERT-a comparative study of transformers language models for the detection of check-worthy claims. In: Working Notes of CLEF (2023)
24. Thorne, J., Vlachos, A., Christodoulopoulos, C., Mittal, A.: Fever: a large-scale dataset for fact extraction and verification. arXiv preprint arXiv:1803.05355 (2018)
25. Touvron, H., et al.: Llama 2: open foundation and fine-tuned chat models. arXiv preprint arXiv:2307.09288 (2023)
26. Wei, J., et al.: Finetuned language models are zero-shot learners (2022)
27. von Werra, L., et al.: TRL: transformer reinforcement learning (2020). https://github.com/huggingface/trl
28. Yang, C., et al.: Large language models as optimizers. arXiv preprint arXiv:2309.03409 (2023)
29. Yang, K.C., Singh, D., Menczer, F.: Characteristics and prevalence of fake social media profiles with AI-generated faces. arXiv preprint arXiv:2401.02627 (2024)

Conspiracy Detection Beyond Text: Exploring the Feasibility of Adding Psycho-Linguistic Features to Enhance Conspiracy Detection Models

Anna R. George[✉], Maximilian Ahrens, Janet B. Pierrehumbert, and Michael McMahon

University of Oxford, Oxford, UK
`anna.george@oii.ox.ac.uk`

Abstract. Conspiracy theories pose a significant societal challenge, particularly online where their spread can be hard to detect. Robust detection models are crucial for effectively identifying these theories. In this study, we investigate incorporating emotional sentiment and moral framing features into a text-based conspiracy detection model. We hypothesize that incorporating these psycho-linguistic elements would enhance the model's performance. Our results reveal significant psycho-linguistic differences between conspiracy and non-conspiracy texts. Conspiracy texts contain higher levels of anger and are framed through the moral lens of cheating, while non-conspiracy texts contain higher levels of joy and are framed through the moral lenses of care and harm. Our model's ability to classify conspiratorial text improves after integrating emotional sentiment and moral framing into the text-based conspiracy detection model. This work demonstrates the potential value of incorporating psycho-linguistic features into text-based models to enhance conspiracy theory detection.

Keywords: Social Science · Computational Social Science · Conspiracy Theories · Classification Models · Moral Foundations Theory

1 Introduction

In today's digital landscape, both factual and misleading narratives significantly influence the dissemination of information across communities. Conspiratorial narratives, in particular, have gained prominence and pose a significant societal challenge. Their spread online is especially problematic, as it can be difficult to detect and counter. Conspiracy theories can undermine public trust, increase societal divisions, and, in some cases, lead to radicalization and extremism.

Given their potential to distort public perception and sow discord, it is urgent to establish methodologies that can effectively detect and classify these narratives as they emerge and spread online. The aim of this paper is to investigate

M. Preuss et al. (Eds.): MISDOOM 2024, LNCS 15175, pp. 32–45, 2024.
https://doi.org/10.1007/978-3-031-71210-4_3

whether incorporating psycho-linguistic features can enhance the performance of text-based conspiracy detection models. Using insights from prior research on the distinguishing linguistic features of conspiracy theories, we endeavor to create and enhance a text-based model's classification abilities by incorporating psycho-linguistic features into the model.

Specifically, we explore the emotional sentiment and moral framing differences between conspiracy and non-conspiracy content, and evaluate whether leveraging these differences can improve automated classification of conspiratorial texts. To achieve this, we develop and compare several conspiracy detection models. We first create a text-based model for conspiracy detection, then create enhanced versions incorporating emotional sentiment and moral framing features. These psycho-linguistic features are detected using custom classifiers we develop and train on open-source datasets. By comparing the performance of these different models, we aim to determine whether, and to what extent, psycho-linguistic features can bolster conspiracy detection capabilities. Our research not only contributes to the understanding of the distinctive psycho-linguistic characteristics of conspiratorial content but also evaluates the potential of incorporating such features to enhance automated conspiracy detection methods.

Our study addresses two main research questions:

Research Question 1 (RQ1): *What are the emotional sentiment and moral framing differences between conspiracy and non-conspiracy tweets?*

Research Question 2 (RQ2): *Can the incorporation of psycho-linguistic features, specifically emotional sentiment and moral framing, improve the performance of text-based conspiracy classification models?*

By answering these questions, we hope to gain insights into the distinctive psycho-linguistic features of conspiratorial content compared to non-conspiratorial content, and evaluate the potential of incorporating such features to enhance conspiracy detection methods.

2   Literature Review

Social scientists define conspiracy theories and conspiratorial thinking in various ways. In our work, we define a conspiracy as an explanation of an event which cites an alternative explanation (e.g., alternative to official accounts) as a salient cause [7]. Lewandowsky and Cook [21] summarized the various aspects of conspiratorial thinking, stating that conspiratorial thinking often includes: contradiction, suspicion, nefarious intent [from the 'official' sources], the feeling that something must be wrong, a persecuted victim (often the person(s) engaging with conspiratorial thinking perceive themselves as the victim(s)), an immunity to evidence, and re-interpreting randomness/random events to fit the conspiracy narrative. Moreover, conspiracies can be characterized by their adversarial undertones [29] and emotive content (e.g., anger) [9].

These beliefs typically arise from a process of radicalization. Online radicalization involves a person progressively engaging with and adopting extremist ideas, leading them to extremist views and, potentially, political violence [28]. The spread of conspiracy theories is accelerated by online platforms, where individuals progressively adopt extremist content [28]. Individuals may shift away from official sources of information as they view themselves as victims being deceived by mainstream narratives [10]. Social media influencers and extremist community leaders exploit these platforms to cultivate their audience, using tactics that contribute to the appeal of alternative movements [22,23].

The process of fringe ideas spreading to mainstream spaces, termed "normiefication" [6], occurs through multiple platforms, with some acting as "bridges" between fringe and mainstream discourse. "Bridge people" with weak ties to multiple groups facilitate the diffusion of information between communities [37]. A study on anti-vaccination conspiracy narratives on Facebook demonstrated the resilience of these narratives, showing that when conspiracy leaders were removed, other conspiracy theorists stepped in to continue spreading the information [25].

While we understand how information spreads through communities and the tactics influencers use to disseminate these narratives, little research has focused on the appeal of the narratives themselves. Given their potential harmful effects, it is crucial to develop effective methods for identifying and understanding these narratives, such as utilizing natural language processing (NLP). NLP is a way of studying language to give it meaningful computational representation [24]. Machine learning can enhance NLP methods to enable researchers to predict psychology traits [36]. A classifier is a machine learning tool that processes the words a person uses to try to decipher the underlying constructs embedded in their words. Until recently, text-based models have been limited by their inability to capture the meaning behind entire sentences and paragraphs. Now, models are able to detect more than the 'keywords' of text, and can encode entire sentences and paragraphs into a meaningful format for NLP tasks. Psychological and linguistic features can be extracted from textual information. These features tend to stem from psychological theory and have previous qualitative and experimental evidence studying their characteristics.

In our study, we classify the content features of moral frames and emotion in conspiratorial text in an attempt to enhance automated classification of conspiracy text. By analyzing these psychological and linguistic features, we hope to gain insights into the distinctive characteristics of conspiratorial content and improve detection methods. Below we review the literature on these features.

2.1   Emotion Detection

Emotions can be described as a multifaceted interplay between subjective experiences and the external world, leading to a range of outcomes: affective experiences such as feelings of happiness or sadness; cognitive processes including judgment and attention focusing; physiological adjustments like increased heart rate or sweating; and expressive behaviors, for example, smiling or frowning [19]. The theory of basic emotions identifies six primary emotions universally expressed and recognized by humans: fear, anger, joy, sadness, disgust, and surprise [8].

Other researchers propose models which organize emotions on two dimensions: pleasure (ranging from misery to pleasure) and arousal (ranging from sleepiness to arousal). This framework allows for a fuller spectrum of emotions, such as: aroused, excited, pleased, sleepy, depressed, miserable, and distressed [33].

Emotion detection involves identifying distinct human emotion types from data sources [30]. Within textual data, emotion detection represents a specialized form of sentiment analysis that extracts fine-grained emotional states from text [1]. Analyzing the words that are being used to communicate not only gives insight into the psychological nature of the person who is expressing the words, but these words can reveal patterns of speech for entire groups of people [18,36].

Various computational approaches are used for analyzing emotional sentiment in text. The Linguistic Inquiry and Word Count (LIWC) utilizes a lexicon-based method to gauge emotional sentiment along with other psychological states [36]. More advanced models, such as those based on transformer models, demonstrate effectiveness in capturing emotional sentiment from complex text structures, outperforming models like GPT-3 [1,3]. In the context of conspiracy theories, prior research indicates that conspiratorial text often expresses emotions like anger and fear [9]. Incorporating emotional insights could potentially enhance the ability to detect conspiracy theories.

2.2   Moral Foundations Theory

According to Moral Foundations Theory (MFT), each person has intuitions that guide their understanding of what is moral and immoral [15]. There are many moral values that may exist and are shared between humans, but the identified and most researched moral values within MFT are: care, respect for authority, purity, fairness, and in-group loyalty. Each value has virtues and vices associated with it. Haidt et al. [15], define the moral value of care as valuing human protection, with the vice acting with cruelty (harm). Respect for authority is an obligation to submit to higher status persons, with the vice (subversion) of disobeying or showing disrespect for authority. Purity is defined as avoiding things that could be deemed disgusting or contaminating, while the vice (degradation) is being degrading or unnatural. Fairness refers to demanding justice, while the vice (cheating) involves injustice or fraud. Lastly, in-group loyalty is defined as being loyal to group affiliations (e.g., nation, family), and the vice (betrayal) is defined as betraying group affiliations [15].

The principles of MFT have been applied in various research contexts, including classification tasks. For instance, [16] leverage MFT to detect polarized concepts in online forums, particularly Reddit. By using text embeddings to project discussions into moral subspaces, the authors capture the nuanced biases in concept discussions, enhancing the detection of ideological polarization without explicit political labels. This demonstrates the potential of using Moral Foundations Theory in classification tasks, especially in the context of online discussions.

The application of MFT in online contexts is particularly relevant given the influence of sentiment on the popularity and diffusion of content. Through studying network diffusion dynamics, researchers find that Twitter (X) messages containing emotional language and moral values that align with the reader are more likely to be shared widely [4]. Conversely, messages that do not align with the reader's moral values are less likely to spread online [4]. Research suggests that individuals who believe in conspiracy theories tend to express the moral values related to purity, authority, and in-group loyalty [20,31]. This could imply that conspiracy messages are often framed with these values in mind, which may in turn facilitate their spread on social media.

Building on these insights, we hypothesize that similar emotional and moral framing differences will be present between conspiracy and non-conspiracy content in our dataset. Therefore, we pose the following research question: (RQ1) *What are the emotional sentiment and moral framing differences between conspiracy and non-conspiracy tweets?*

2.3   Enhanced Conspiracy Detection

The transmission of conspiracy theories poses a significant concern given their potential to undermine public trust and increase societal divisions [35]. Quickly, and accurately, identifying conspiracy theories allows for proactive measures to limit their spread, thereby preserving public trust and providing accurate information to the public. Although there are some examples of research combining psychological features with textual data to enhance conspiracy detection, these are limited. There are also limited instances in other fields where psychological features and textual embeddings are integrated, such as in personality prediction using social media data [5]. However, the creation of models that integrate text and psycho-linguistic features is relatively unexplored, especially in the field of conspiracy detection. The closest related work involves using psycho-linguistic features along with convolutional neural networks (CNNs) to identify individuals who propagate conspiracy theories [13].

Our research seeks to fill this gap by incorporating psycho-linguistic features into a transformer model to improve conspiracy theory detection. This model combines textual embeddings with the psycho-linguistic features of emotional sentiment and moral frames to classify texts as conspiratorial or non-conspiratorial. This integration aims to leverage the strengths of both psycho-linguistic features and text analysis techniques with the aim of creating a more accurate conspiracy detection model. Given this, we ask: (RQ2) *Can the incorporation of psycho-linguistic features, specifically emotional sentiment and moral framing, improve the performance of text-based conspiracy classification models?*

3   Methodology

3.1   Datasets

We use open-sourced datasets to train and evaluate our classification models. To work with the data, we first clean the text before training the model. During the text pre-processing, we remove URLs, symbols, and numerals from the dataset, and convert all the text data to lowercase as these elements can introduce noise when working with text-based information.

We use the Emotion Dataset ($n = 416{,}809$) [34] to train our emotion detection model. Each tweet is annotated with theoretically derived emotions, inferred from the hashtags used within the tweet. These hashtags are then removed during the training and testing process.

To explore the moral framing of online content, we incorporate three resources: the Moral Foundations Dictionary 2.0 ($n = 2{,}041$ unique keywords, Frimer et al., 2019), Moral Foundation Twitter (X) Corpus ($n = 1{,}386$, Hoover et al., 2019), and the Moral Sentiment Reddit dataset ($n = 500$, George et al., 2020). These datasets contain keywords and social media posts annotated for moral expression. The Reddit dataset [12] contains Reddit posts from four sub-Reddits (r/LateStageCapitalism, r/liberal, r/Conservative, and r/The_Donald. Posts are collected in relation to four political issues (migration, abortion, climate change, and gun rights). Each Reddit post in the dataset undergoes manual coding. Annotations are made based on the virtues, vices, or absence of moral values aligned with Moral Foundations Theory.

The MFT dictionary 2.0 [11] is an enhanced version of the original MFT dictionary [14], both of which provide a list words related to each moral value. To validate this revised list's relevance to the intended moral values, [11] conduct a study involving participants from a diverse set of countries, including Spain, Egypt, Moldova, India, the United States, and Venezuela. Participants are prompted to write paragraphs that reflect specific moral values, allowing the researchers to assess the dictionary's accuracy by comparing these paragraphs to the list of keywords. The MFT Twitter (X) Corpus is an open sourced collection of hand coded moral values for several different topics [17]. Each tweet in the corpus is coded for moral values by 3 to 4 annotators. Each annotator hand codes tweets for the presence of moral values or the absence of any of the values.

We retrieve conspiracy tweets from a multi-topic conspiracy dataset ($n = 3{,}100$) [32]. The dataset is comprised of a collection of tweets specifically related to conspiracy theories about climate change, Covid-19, and Jeffrey Epstein. This dataset is hand-labeled by the researchers with a binary variable denoting the presence or absence of a conspiracy theory within the tweet. We collect the tweets for this dataset using the tweet IDs and the v.1 Twitter (X) API. We were able to obtain 1,558 tweets from the original dataset.

3.2   Emotion Detection Classifier

The base of our emotion detection classifier is the pre-trained RoBERTa language model [26]. Using transfer learning, we fine-tune RoBERTa to detect emotional sentiment by training RoBERTa on the Emotion Dataset [34], which contains 416,809 tweets labeled with one of six emotions (anger, fear, joy, love, sadness, and surprise). In the dataset, each tweet is annotated with one emotion, inferred from the hashtags used within the tweet. The dataset is divided into an 80:20 train-test split. To fine-tune the model, we use the AdamW optimizer [27] and cross-entropy loss during training. Early stopping is used to prevent overfitting. The early stopping logic is implemented by monitoring the F1-score across epochs and terminating training if performance does not improve for 2 epochs.

The best model state for the epoch with the highest f1-score is saved. The final version of the model is then run on the test dataset, and results in an overall F1 score of 0.940. The precision, recall, and F1 score values for each emotion also show the model is able to accurately detect emotions within the text. The scores for each emotion are shown in Table 1.

Table 1. Precision, Recall, and F1 Scores for the Emotion Detection Model

Emotion	Precision	Recall	F1 Score
Anger	0.95	0.95	0.95
Fear	0.87	0.94	0.91
Joy	0.92	0.99	0.96
Love	0.99	0.71	0.83
Sadness	0.98	0.98	0.98
Surprise	0.99	0.64	0.78

3.3   Moral Framing Classifier

We develop a classifier to detect the moral framing in conspiratorial posts. The classifier is developed using similar techniques to the emotional sentiment classifier, where RoBERTa is trained to classify moral framing by learning moral frames from hand coded textual data (as has been seen in previous research [12]). After combining the MFT dictionary 2.0 [11], MFT Twitter (X) Elections Corpus [17], and MFT Reddit corpus [12] (total $n = 3,927$), the training and evaluation data are split by a conventional 80:20 split. The cut-off score for labeling a value as present or not-present is set to the high standard of 0.90. The classifier performs well, with a high success rate of accurately classifying the data (Label ranking average precision $= 0.997$, evaluation loss $= 0.012$). Table 2 shows precision, recall, and F1 score for each value.

3.4   Conspiracy Detection Classifiers

To answer the first research question, we create a conspiracy detection classifier based on the multi-topic conspiracy dataset [32]. The model base is RoBERTa. We split the dataset into an 80:10:10 split of training, testing, and validation respectively.

All models are trained using the AdamW optimizer [27] with a learning rate of 4e−5 and the binary cross-entropy loss function. To handle the class imbalance in the training data, with more conspiracy tweets ($n = 935$) than non-conspiracy tweets ($n = 311$), we incorporate class weights into the loss function. These weights are inversely proportional to the class frequencies, assigning a higher weight to the minority non-conspiracy class. This approach encourages the model

Table 2. Precision, Recall, and F1 Scores for Moral Framing Model

Category	Precision	Recall	F1 Score
Care	0.99	0.96	0.97
Harm	0.99	0.99	0.99
Fairness	0.99	0.99	0.99
Cheating	1.00	1.00	1.00
Loyalty	0.96	0.96	0.96
Betrayal	0.98	0.98	0.98
Authority	1.00	0.98	0.99
Subversion	0.99	1.00	1.00
Purity	0.99	1.00	1.00
Degradation	1.00	0.96	0.98

to focus more on correctly identifying the underrepresented non-conspiracy class, rather than being biased towards simply predicting the majority conspiracy class by penalizing the model more for mistakes on the minority class. By penalizing mistakes on the minority class more heavily, the training process is incentivized to better represent both classes. The training process is performed over 30 epochs, with early stopping implemented if the model does not improve after 5 epochs to prevent overfitting. After each epoch, the model is evaluated on the validation set, and the best-performing model is saved.

To evaluate the impact of different features, we develop several models: a text-only baseline, models integrating text with emotion or moral frames, and a combined model with both text, emotions, and moral frames. The emotion-based detection model extends the text-only model by introducing an emotion embedding layer that transforms categorical emotion data into a continuous, fixed-size vector. These emotion vectors are concatenated with the output from the RoBERTa model's first token so that both the emotions and textual information are integrated into the model. The models which include moral frames have a similar architecture but differ in the type of data used. Unlike the categorical emotions, moral frames are represented as continuous scores ranging from 0 to 1, reflecting the strength or presence of each moral frame in the text. These scores are directly concatenated with the RoBERTa output.

Figure 1 illustrates a simplified version of the conspiracy classification process. Suppose the input tweet is "The government is lying about the COVID-19 vaccines to control us!" In the Input Layer, the tokenized textual data is processed. In the Processing Layer, the tweet is transformed into a RoBERTa embedding, converting the text into a numerical format using the RoBERTa language model. Additionally, psycho-linguistic features are converted into

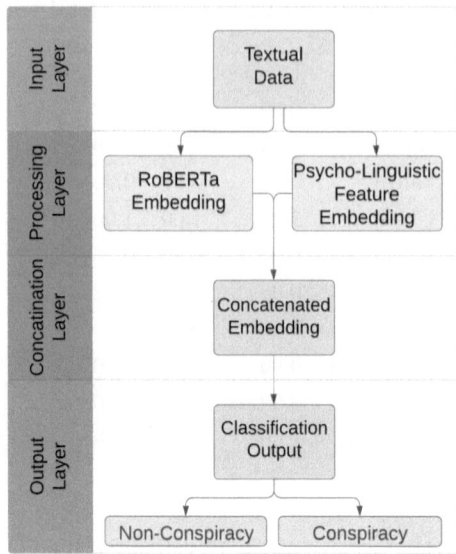

Fig. 1. Conspiracy Detection Model Architecture

embeddings representing either emotions or moral frames. These embeddings are then combined in the Concatenation Layer into a single feature vector. Finally, in the Output Layer, the combined features are processed by the classifier to determines whether the tweet is classified as "Conspiracy" or "Non-Conspiracy."

4   Results

4.1   Research Question 1: What Are the Emotional Sentiment and Moral Framing Differences Between Conspiracy and Non-conspiracy Tweets?

Emotional Differences. To classify the emotional sentiment in conspiracy tweets we use our emotion detection model. Our model outputs a probability score for each possible emotion, which represents the model's confidence that a given emotion is the most appropriate label for the text. Due to the original dataset always having an emotion label, we need to introduce the label of "no emotion". Therefore, we set a cut-off score to indicate how high the probability needs to be to label the emotion as present in the text. We choose the cut-off score based on the mean of the distribution of probability scores ($M = 0.640$). Texts are labeled with emotion with the highest probability score as long as that probability score is above 0.640, while those with scores under this threshold are considered emotionless.

Running the model on the multi-topic conspiracy dataset [32] we apply a Chi-square test for independence to evaluate emotional differences between tweets containing or not containing conspiracies. The results indicate a significant overall variation in the distribution of emotions between the two groups ($\chi^2(6, n = 1{,}558)$: 15.536, $p = 0.017$). Post hoc Z-tests for individual emotions reveal that anger is significantly more common in conspiracy-related texts ($p < 0.01$), while joy is more common in non-conspiracy related texts than conspiracy related texts ($p < 0.05$). Fear, love, sadness, and surprise do not differ significantly between groups ($p > 0.05$).

Moral Framing Differences. Similar to emotional sentiment differences, we also look at the differences in moral framing by conspiracy type in the multi-topic conspiracy dataset. To classify the moral framing in tweets we use our moral framing detection model. Our model outputs a probability score for each possible moral value, which represents the model's confidence that a given value frame is used in the text. The distribution of probability scores peaks around 0 and on the upper end towards 1, so a cut-off score of 0.90 is applied. Running the model on the multi-topic conspiracy dataset [32] we apply a Chi-square test for independence to evaluate moral framing differences between tweets containing or not containing conspiracies.

The results indicate a significant variation in the distribution of moral frames between conspiracy and non-conspiracy tweets ($\chi^2(9, n = 1{,}558) = 34.584, p < 0.001$). Post hoc Z-tests for individual moral values indicate care ($p < 0.001$) and harm ($p = 0.004$) are more prevalent in non-conspiracy texts than conspiracy tweets, while Cheating is significantly more common in conspiracy-related tweets than in non-conspiracy related texts ($p < 0.001$). Other moral values such as fairness, loyalty, betrayal, authority, subversion, purity, and degradation do not show significant differences between the groups ($p > 0.05$).

4.2 Research Question 2: Can the Incorporation of Psycho-Linguistic Features, Specifically Emotional Sentiment and Moral Framing, Improve the Performance of Text-Based Conspiracy Classification Models?

To address research question 2, we build several conspiracy classification models as described in the methods section. After establishing a text-only RoBERTa conspiracy classifier as a baseline, we evaluate the impact of integrating different psycho-linguistic features related to emotions and moral framing.

The results show that incorporating all 6 emotion features boosts the F1 scores on both the validation and test sets compared to the text-only model. Given the significant differences in anger and joy between conspiracy and non-conspiracy texts observed in RQ1, we also try adding only those specific emotion features. Indeed, adding only the anger feature to the text-based model shows an improvement in the model over the text-based model alone. Similarly, the combination of joy and the text-based information improves performance over the text-based model alone, though to a lesser extent than anger.

A similar pattern is observed for moral framing features. Incorporating all 10 moral frames shows slight improvement over the text-only model. Given the significant differences in cheating, care, and harm between conspiracy and non-conspiracy texts observed in RQ1, we try adding only those specific moral frames as features. In these instances, a more substantial improvement is observed when combining these specific moral values with the text-based model than when all 10 moral frames are included in the model. Most notably, adding both care and harm to text-based features results in the best performing model in the testing dataset, while adding all three moral frames of cheating, care, and harm results in the best model in the validation dataset. Table 3 presents the full results across these models on the validation and test datasets.

Table 3. Results of the multi-topic conspiracy detection model

Model	F1 Score (Validation)	F1 Score (Test)
Emotions	0.683	0.730
Moral Frames	0.483	0.607
Text (RoBERTa)	0.817	0.781
Text (RoBERTa) + Emotions	0.829	0.858
Text (RoBERTa) + Joy	0.836	0.856
Text (RoBERTa) + Anger	0.832	0.879
Text (RoBERTa) + Joy + Anger	0.809	0.840
Text (RoBERTa) + Moral Frames	0.823	0.800
Text (RoBERTa) + Cheating	0.814	0.826
Text (RoBERTa) + Harm	0.832	0.891
Text (RoBERTa) + Care	0.821	0.872
Text (RoBERTa) + Cheating + Care	0.814	0.892
Text (RoBERTa) + Cheating + Harm	0.829	0.889
Text (RoBERTa) + Care + Harm	0.820	**0.895**
Text (RoBERTa) + Cheating + Care + Harm	**0.843**	0.874

5   Conclusion

In this study, we investigate the psycho-linguistic differences between conspiracy and non-conspiracy texts, and if these differences can be incorporated into a conspiracy detection model to improve classification performance. The results reveal significant differences between conspiracy and non-conspiracy texts in our dataset. Consistent with previous research [9], we found that conspiracy narratives express higher anger sentiment. However, contrary to existing literature, our conspiracy texts did not exhibit higher fear sentiment [9] or emphasize moral frames like purity or loyalty [20,31]. Instead, conspiracy texts in our dataset prominently featured moral frames related to cheating. Non-conspiracy narratives, conversely, tended to express more joy and highlight moral concerns around care and harm avoidance. These differences may be attributed due to our dataset's broader range of conspiracy topics, suggesting that emotional and moral patterns in conspiracy theories could be topic-specific. Future research could explore how these patterns vary across different conspiracy theories.

Importantly, our results demonstrate that integrating specific psycho-linguistic features related to emotions and moral framing can significantly enhance the accuracy of text-based conspiracy detection models. Incorporating features such as anger sentiment and moral framing around cheating, harm, and care substantially improved our models' predictive performance. These findings have crucial implications for content moderation strategies on social media platforms, potentially enabling more effective identification and mitigation of harmful conspiracy theories.

However, our study has limitations. Our emotion detection relies solely on textual content, lacking access to non-verbal communicative signals that could aid in emotion recognition [2]. Additionally, while our dataset covers multiple conspiracy topics, it may not be representative of all conspiracy theories circulating online and is limited to one platform (i.e., Twitter/X). Future research should aim to validate our findings using larger and more diverse datasets, explore the effectiveness of incorporating other psycho-linguistic features, and investigate if conspiracies are expressed differently on other platforms. Furthermore, examining how emotional and moral patterns vary across different conspiracy theory topics could provide valuable insights into the nature and spread of these narratives.

Nevertheless, our work illustrates the potential of incorporating psycho-linguistic features to enhance conspiracy detection models. As conspiracy theories proliferate in the digital age, developing robust detection methods that leverage insights from multiple disciplines is crucial in combating their spread and societal impact. Our study contributes to this important goal, and our improved detection model could facilitate more timely identification and intervention, potentially mitigating the harmful effects of conspiracy theories on public discourse, trust, and decision-making. This interdisciplinary approach underscores the necessity of integrating diverse fields to address the complex challenges posed by online conspiracy theories.

Acknowledgments. The research was funded by the Alan Turing Institute and the UK Defence Science and Technology Laboratory, European Research Council (Consolidator Grant Agreement 819131), and The Dieter Schwarz Foundation.

Disclosure of Interests. The authors have no competing interests to declare that are relevant to the content of this article.

References

1. Acheampong, F.A., Nunoo-Mensah, H., Chen, W.: Transformer models for text-based emotion detection: a review of BERT-based approaches. Artif. Intell. Rev. **54**(8), 5789–5829 (2021)
2. Beattie, G.W.: Language and non-verbal communication: the essential synthesis. Linguistics **19**, 1165–1183 (1981)
3. Boitel, E., Mohasseb, A., Haig, E.: A comparative analysis of GPT-3 and BERT models for text-based emotion recognition: performance, efficiency, and robustness. In: Naik, N., Jenkins, P., Grace, P., Yang, L., Prajapat, S. (eds.) UK Workshop on Computational Intelligence, pp. 567–579. Springer, Cham (2023). https://doi.org/10.1007/978-3-031-47508-5_44
4. Brady, W.J., Wills, J.A., Jost, J.T., Tucker, J.A., Van Bavel, J.J.: Emotion shapes the diffusion of moralized content in social networks. Proc. Natl. Acad. Sci. **114**(28), 7313–7318 (2017). https://doi.org/10.1073/pnas.1618923114
5. Christian, H., Suhartono, D., Chowanda, A., Zamli, K.Z.: Text based personality prediction from multiple social media data sources using pre-trained language model and model averaging. J. Big Data **8**(1), 68 (2021)
6. De Zeeuw, D., Hagen, S., Peeters, S., Jokubauskaite, E.: Tracing normiefication. First Monday (2020). https://doi.org/10.5210/fm.v25i11.10643
7. Dentith, M.R.: The philosophy of conspiracy theory: bringing the epistemology of a freighted term into the social sciences (2018)
8. Ekman, P.: Are there basic emotions? (1992)
9. Fong, A., Roozenbeek, J., Goldwert, D., Rathje, S., van der Linden, S.: The language of conspiracy: a psychological analysis of speech used by conspiracy theorists and their followers on Twitter. Group Process. Intergroup Relat. **24**(4), 606–623 (2021)
10. Franks, B., Bangerter, A., Bauer, M.W.: Conspiracy theories as quasi-religious mentality: an integrated account from cognitive science, social representations theory, and frame theory. Front. Psychol. **4**, 424 (2013)
11. Frimer, J.A., Boghrati, R., Haidt, J., Graham, J., Dehgani, M.: Moral foundations dictionary for linguistic analyses 2.0 (2019). https://doi.org/10.17605/OSF.IO/EZN37
12. George, A., Bright, J.: Classifying moral sentiment to measure differences in online political self-expression. Thesis (MSC), University of Oxford (2020)
13. Giachanou, A., Ghanem, B., Rosso, P.: Detection of conspiracy propagators using psycho-linguistic characteristics. J. Inf. Sci. **49**(1), 3–17 (2023)
14. Graham, J., Haidt, J., Nosek, B.: Liberals and conservatives rely on different sets of moral foundations. J. Pers. Soc. Psychol. **96**(5), 1029–1046 (2009). https://doi.org/10.1037/a0015141
15. Haidt, J., Joseph, C.: Intuitive ethics: how innately prepared intuitions generate culturally variable virtues. Daedalus **133**(4), 55–66 (2004)
16. Hofmann, V., Dong, X., Pierrehumbert, J.B., Schütze, H.: Modeling ideological salience and framing in polarized online groups with graph neural networks and structured sparsity. arXiv preprint arXiv:2104.08829 (2021)
17. Hoover, J., et al.: Moral foundations Twitter corpus: a collection of 35k tweets annotated for moral sentiment. Soc. Psychol. Pers. Sci. **11**, 1057–1071 (2019). https://doi.org/10.1177/1948550619876629
18. Khalid, O., Srinivasan, P.: Style matters! Investigating linguistic style in online communities. In: Proceedings of the International AAAI Conference on Web and Social Media, vol. 14, pp. 360–369. AAAI (2020)

19. Kleinginna, P.R., Jr., Kleinginna, A.M.: A categorized list of emotion definitions, with suggestions for a consensual definition. Motiv. Emot. **5**(4), 345–379 (1981)
20. Leone, L., Giacomantonio, M., Lauriola, M.: Moral foundations, worldviews, moral absolutism and belief in conspiracy theories. Int. J. Psychol. **54**(2), 197–204 (2019)
21. Lewandowsky, S., Cook, J.: The Conspiracy Theory Handbook (2020)
22. Lewis, B.: Alternative influence. Technical report, Data & Society; Data & Society Research Institute (2018)
23. Lewis, R.: "This is What the News Won't Show You": YouTube creators and the reactionary politics of micro-celebrity. Telev. New Media **21**(2), 201–217 (2020). https://doi.org/10.1177/1527476419879919
24. Liddy, E.: Natural language processing. In: Encyclopedia of Library and Information Science, 2 edn. Marcel Decker, Inc., New York (2001)
25. Ligot, D., Tayco, F.C., Toledo, M., Nazareno, C., Brennan-Rieder, D.: Infodemiology: computational methodologies for quantifying and visualizing key characteristics of the COVID-19 infodemic. SSRN Electron. J. (2021). https://doi.org/10.2139/ssrn.3771695
26. Liu, Y., et al.: RoBERTa: a robustly optimized BERT pretraining approach. arXiv preprint arXiv:1907.11692 (2019)
27. Loshchilov, I., Hutter, F.: Decoupled weight decay regularization. arXiv preprint arXiv:1711.05101 (2017)
28. Marwick, A.E., Furl, K.: Taking the Redpill: talking about extremism. AoIR Selected Papers of Internet Research (2021)
29. Moffitt, J.D., King, C.: Hunting conspiracy theories during the COVID-19 pandemic. Soc. Media + Soc. **7**(3), 20563051211043212 (2021)
30. Nandwani, P., Verma, R.: A review on sentiment analysis and emotion detection from text. Soc. Netw. Anal. Min. **11**(1), 81 (2021)
31. Nejat, P., Heirani-Tabas, A., Nazarpour, M.M.: Moral foundations are better predictors of belief in Covid-19 conspiracy theories than the big five personality traits. Front. Psychol. **14**, 1201695 (2023)
32. Phillips, S.C., Ng, L.H.X., Carley, K.M.: Hoaxes and Hidden agendas: a Twitter conspiracy theory dataset: data paper. In: Companion Proceedings of the Web Conference 2022, pp. 876–880, April 2022
33. Russell, J.A.: A circumplex model of affect. J. Pers. Soc. Psychol. **39**(6), 1161 (1980)
34. Saravia, E., Liu, H.C.T., Huang, Y.H., Wu, J., Chen, Y.S.: CARER: contextualized affect representations for emotion recognition. In: Proceedings of the 2018 Conference on Empirical Methods in Natural Language Processing, pp. 3687–3697. Association for Computational Linguistics, Brussels, Belgium, October–November 2018. https://doi.org/10.18653/v1/D18-1404
35. Sunstein, C.R., Vermeule, A.: Conspiracy theories: causes and cures. J Polit Philos **17**(2), 202–227 (2009)
36. Tausczik, Y.R., Pennebaker, J.W.: The psychological meaning of words: LIWC and computerized text analysis methods. J. Lang. Soc. Psychol. **29**(1), 24–54 (2010)
37. Zhao, J., Wu, J., Xu, K.: Weak ties: subtle role of information diffusion in online social networks. Phys. Rev. E **82**, 016105 (2010)

To Share or Not to Share: Randomized Controlled Study of Misinformation Warning Labels on Social Media

Anatoliy Gruzd[1]([⊠]), Philip Mai[1], and Felipe B. Soares[2]

[1] Toronto Metropolitan University, Ted Rogers School of Management, Social Media Lab,
Toronto, Canada
gruzd@torontomu.ca
[2] University of the Arts London, London College of Communications, London, UK

Abstract. Can warning labels on social media posts reduce the spread of misinformation online? This paper presents the results of an empirical study using ModSimulator, an open-source mock social media research tool, to test the effectiveness of soft moderation interventions aimed at limiting misinformation spread and informing users about post accuracy. Specifically, the study used ModSimulator to create a social media interface that mimics the experience of using Facebook and tested two common soft moderation interventions – a footnote warning label and a blur filter – to examine how users (n = 1500) respond to misinformation labels attached to false claims about the Russia-Ukraine war. Results indicate that both types of interventions decreased engagement with posts featuring false claims in a Facebook-like simulated interface, with neither demonstrating a significantly stronger effect than the other. In addition, the study finds that belief in pro-Kremlin claims and trust in partisan sources increase the likelihood of engagement, while trust in fact-checking organizations and frequent commenting on Facebook lowers it. These findings underscore the importance of not solely relying on soft moderation interventions, as other factors impact users' decisions to engage with misinformation on social media.

Keywords: Misinformation Interventions · Warning Labels · Content Moderation · Platform Governance · Facebook · Fact-checks · Russia-Ukraine War

1 Introduction

Around the world, people are turning to social media platforms such as TikTok, Facebook, Instagram, X, Mastodon and many others to stay connected, get news, and share thoughts and ideas. As a result of its ubiquity, social media has emerged as a major conduit for the spread of misinformation. However, corporations that own these platforms are often reluctant to remove posts containing false information, fearing a potential decline in engagement or charges of censorship. Instead, they tend to opt for less restrictive interventions, such as appending warning labels to posts that have been independently

© The Author(s) 2024
M. Preuss et al. (Eds.): MISDOOM 2024, LNCS 15175, pp. 46–69, 2024.
https://doi.org/10.1007/978-3-031-71210-4_4

fact-checked or linking to verified sources of information. These interventions, often called "soft moderation", aim to inform users rather than completely restrict access to content.

This study aims to investigate the effectiveness of soft moderation interventions in reducing the spread of misinformation on social media platforms. Although platforms frequently experiment with such interventions in real-world settings, the public often lacks access to the results of these internal tests. Furthermore, even when results are publicly disclosed, the need for transparency and independent audits remains. This need arises from the inherent conflict of interest between the goals of social media companies to prioritize engagement and monetization over their responsibilities to prevent their platform from being used for spreading misinformation and inciting violence.

Previous research has found mixed results when testing the effectiveness of different interventions against misinformation. Some studies found that interventions, including soft moderation techniques, can reduce the intention of sharing misinformation or the perceived accuracy of false claims [1–4]. Other studies found that some interventions have limited effectiveness [5, 6] and might even backfire, making people less likely to trust reliable sources [7], or more likely to believe in false claims [8]. Due to conflicting evidence regarding the effectiveness of interventions, further research in this area is still necessary. Moreover, there exists a methodological gap in studies on soft moderation, with many not conducted in an ecologically valid setting and relying either on self-reported data to study behavioural intentions or observed data about specific case studies on social media.

To keep the study focused and relevant to current events, we examined and tested the effectiveness of soft moderation interventions (i.e., footnote warning labels and blur filters) on claims about the ongoing Russia-Ukraine war that had been rated as "false" by independent fact-checkers. This case was chosen because it has been shown to attract misinformation as each side competes to create a more favourable information environment for their agenda.

The Kremlin has a long history of engaging in disinformation campaigns in Russia and worldwide [9]. In recent years, these campaigns have focused on spreading false and misleading claims about the Russia-Ukraine war, often to undermine support for Ukraine [10, 11]. As this study is conducted in Canada, we examine if and how Canadians engage with common misinformation about the war, known to be propagated by Kremlin and pro-Kremlin accounts on social media and targeting audiences in the West [9, 12, 13].

2 Previous Work

Misinformation is broadly defined as incorrect, misleading, or unproven claims presented as facts. When misinformation is created to support an agenda - that is, when the incorrect, misleading or unproven claim is made to mislead others and potentially manipulate public opinion - it is called disinformation [14]. Given that it is not always possible to determine if a piece of misinformation was shared to deceive, we will use the broader term 'misinformation' throughout this paper.

There are five general categories of interventions against misinformation [15]: 1) Boosting, which focuses on increasing knowledge and media literacy so that individuals can spot and deal with misinformation; 2) Inoculation, which uses pre-bunking strategies that include warning people about misinformation and exposing people to misinformation in a controlled environment so that they learn how to identify misinformation in real life; 3) Identity Management, which focuses on reducing individual bias in the process of selecting and evaluating information (e.g., asking the individual to think of themselves in the place of other people); 4) Nudging, which provides incentives for individuals exposed to misinformation, such as accuracy and credibility nudges; and, 5) Fact-checking, which uses techniques such as flagging misinformation and providing corrections from experts.

Studies that tested boosting interventions reported conflicting results. For example, [6] found that a pedagogical intervention based on media literacy training to combat misinformation did not significantly change participants' ability to identify misinformation. Similarly, [16] discovered that the boosting intervention, which included using an infographic to teach how to verify information, did not significantly change the belief accuracy of participants about the COVID-19 pandemic. In contrast, [7] found that a digital media literacy intervention reduced the perceived accuracy of false news headlines. Yet, another study [8] found that boosting interventions backfired. The authors tested three boosting interventions intended to address anti-vaccine beliefs; none showed effectiveness in reducing anti-vaccine beliefs, and two of the three led to increased misperceptions about vaccines. However, in a more recent replication study [17], none of the conditions previously tested in [8] showed an increase in vaccine misconceptions. Differences in findings are likely due to variations in how the boosting strategy was implemented and other factors in the experimental designs of these studies.

Studies evaluating inoculation interventions found more consistent and promising results. [18–20] tested a pre-bunking intervention using online games against COVID-19 misinformation. All three studies found that the game-based intervention increased participants' capacity to perceive COVID-19 misinformation as manipulative, improved confidence in their ability to spot misinformation, and reduced their self-reported willingness to share misinformation. Another study [21] exposed participants to conspiracy theories about vaccines and anti-conspiracy arguments. The authors found that exposing people to anti-conspiracy arguments before exposing them to conspiracy theories reduced the likelihood of participants believing in them. Conversely, exposing participants to anti-conspiracy arguments after they were exposed to conspiracy theories was ineffective in reducing conspiracy beliefs.

Studies focusing on identity management interventions are still rare [15]. In one of the few, [22] asked participants to reflect on their values in a self-affirmation exercise before asking about their beliefs in vaccine safety and intention to vaccinate children. They found no evidence that the identity management intervention would effectively reduce anti-vaccine attitudes. Similarly, [23] tested the effectiveness of self-affirmation exercises in reducing misperceptions and increasing willingness to accept corrective information. The authors found no significant effect for the latter and only limited evidence for the former.

Studies that focused on nudging interventions also found mixed results. [24] tested how shifting attention to accuracy can reduce the intention to share misinformation. They found that asking participants to rate the accuracy of a single non-partisan news headline at the outset of the study decreased participants' intention to share misinformation. On the other hand, [5] tested the impact of source credibility labels embedded in users' social feeds and search results pages. The authors found it ineffective at reducing consumption of unreliable sources, belief in misinformation, or changing trust levels in the media.

Research focused on fact-checking interventions is particularly relevant to our study since it includes soft-moderation techniques, such as flagging misinformation and providing additional information we test in our work. Previous research has assessed the effectiveness of soft interventions to reduce the spread of misinformation on social media primarily by using 1) self-reported data from experiments and surveys about the perceived accuracy and willingness to share social media posts and 2) observed data by tracking interactions on social media platforms.

Relying on self-reported data, [4] found that attaching warnings to headlines of news stories disputed by fact-checkers reduced the perceived accuracy and intention to share these stories. However, the authors also found that warnings caused untagged false headlines to be perceived as more accurate. [1] found that adding general warnings or specific "Disputed" or "Rated false" tags decreased the perceived accuracy of misleading information on social media. Additionally, the authors found that adding the more direct tag "Rated false" to a post lowers its perceived accuracy more than a "Disputed" tag. [25] tested the effectiveness of inserting warning tags and warning covers in tweets containing misinformation in changing the perceived accuracy of misleading statements. They found that only tweets with warning covers significantly changed the perceived accuracy of misinformation.

In terms of observed data, [2] found that even adding a simple prompt on TikTok videos with potentially misleading information reminding users to think about its accuracy reduced the number of shares on the platform by 24% and likes by 7%. Two separate studies [3] and [26] analyzed Trump's tweets about the 2020 U.S. election. [3] found that, overall, the placement of soft moderation labels did not change the propensity of users to share and engage with labeled content. However, labels that directly refuted the false claim from a tweet were associated with fewer user interactions with false content. On the other hand, [26] found that soft moderation had a backfire effect and increased the spread of tweets with warning labels.

A major limitation of most previous research is the absence of an ecologically valid setting when testing the effectiveness of soft moderation interventions. Consequently, these studies were restricted to studying the effects of social media misinformation interventions on behavioral intentions (e.g., intention to share) rather than on observed behavior (e.g., sharing). This is a further limitation as some work has shown that behavioral intentions may not always align with actual behavior [27]. To address this limitation, our study builds on previous research by including interaction with two soft moderation interventions in an ecologically valid setting during a survey. More specifically, in addition to measuring respondents' perceptions (self-reported data) about their belief in certain types of misinformation, we also study their behavior in an environment that simulates the experience of using a social media platform, specifically Facebook, as it is the most popular platform in Canada [28].

3   Research Questions

3.1   Do Soft Moderation Interventions Commonly Used by Social Media Platforms Reduce Engagement with Misinformation? (RQ1)

To answer this question, we tested the effectiveness of two soft moderation interventions: 1) a footnote label at the bottom of a post that has been previously flagged as "False Information" by independent fact-checkers, and 2) a blur filter with a "False Information" warning that covers a post that has been fact-checked as "False". The latter intervention allows users to see and engage with the fact-checked post, but only after reading and acknowledging the warning. We focus on these two interventions because they are commonly used on Facebook. It is also the most popular social media platform for news consumption among Canadians, with 40% of the population using it [29]. Furthermore, Facebook has been shown to be particularly popular among Canadians for getting news about the Russia-Ukraine war, with 33% of the population reporting using it for this purpose [12].

3.2   What User-Specific Factors Can Predict Users' Engagement with Misinformation? (RQ2)

In addition to testing the impact of the interventions on user engagement with misinformation, we need to consider other factors that may also influence user behavior when faced with misinformation. To answer RQ2, we measured and tested factors that prior literature found associated with one's willingness to share or believe in misinformation. These include news and media consumption habits, political ideology, populist attitude, frequency of social media use, and demographic variables (age and gender) [30–33]. Below is a brief review of relevant factors and corresponding literature.

Trust in News Media. [34] conducted a longitudinal survey in Chile between 2017 and 2019, finding that skepticism of mainstream news media was associated with belief in misinformation. [31] surveyed the U.S. population during the 2016 U.S. Presidential election, finding that trust in partisan media outlets was associated with belief in misinformation.

Trust in Governments. When examining trust towards a particular government, [35] found that Brazilians who trusted President Bolsonaro's administration were more likely to believe in electoral misinformation after the country's 2022 election. [36] found that Canadians who were more likely to trust the Russian government were also more likely to believe misinformation about the Russia-Ukraine war. In contrast, the authors found that trusting the Ukrainian government reduced the chance of believing misinformation related to the war.

Trust in Fact-Checking. Since the tested interventions are based on the fact-checks done by professional and independent organizations, it is essential to examine a potential relationship between trust in fact-checking organizations and belief in, or engagement with, misinformation. The perceived credibility of a source (in our case, a fact-checking organization) plays an important role in influencing the perceived credibility of information - that is, a warning label [37]. Thus, we expect trust in fact-checking organizations to limit engagement with misinformation. However, prior research on this topic is limited and contradictory. For example, [38] found that approximately a third of their survey participants (n = 8235) in Australia would likely engage with misinformation despite trusting a fact-check.

Political Ideology and Populism. A right-leaning political ideology is associated with belief in pro-Kremlin misinformation [36], and conservatism predicts susceptibility to COVID-19 misinformation [39]. Another study [40] examined a related concept - political populism - and found its association with belief in COVID-19 conspiracy theories and misinformation.

Social Media Use. Social media use, specifically its frequent use, has shown a positive association with believing in misinformation. [30] found that frequent users are more likely to believe in conspiracy theories and misinformation.

Prior Beliefs. Previous studies have shown that users' prior beliefs affect what claims they believe [41]. However, prior beliefs are often overlooked in this line of research [42]. Considering the focus of this study, we are interested in testing the relationship between users' prior beliefs in pro-Kremlin claims and their engagement with false claims.

Demographic Variables. Age and gender have often been shown to predict one's propensity to share or believe misinformation. For example, older adults are less likely to verify suspicious content [43] and more likely to share misinformation [44]. In contrast, younger individuals are more worried about encountering misinformation [45]. Gender has been shown to have a statistically significant but relatively small effect on people's concern about misinformation, with men only 5% more concerned than women [45].

4 Methods

Before data collection was initiated, the study protocol was reviewed and approved by the University Research Ethics Board. Once the ethics approval was received, we recruited 1500 Facebook users (18+) in Canada. We used the Facebook Ads platform to get an estimate for a representative sample based on gender, age, and location. Since Facebook provides the minimum and maximum estimates for each category, we used the average of the two to calculate the targeted number of responses (see Table A.1 in Appendix A). Participants were recruited using Dynata, a market research company.

Study Environment. A key feature of our method is the implementation and use of a new interactive research tool called ModSimulator to test the effectiveness of soft moderation interventions on social media [46]. The ModSimulator is an extension of the Mock Social Media Website (MSMW) tool, an open-source package designed to conduct experimental research on social media behavior [47]. With the ModSimulator, researchers can create a customized, interactive social media feed that resembles a Facebook interface, enabling them to add fact-check footnotes or blur screens to selected posts in the simulated feed. Figure 1 highlights custom elements introduced to display fact-checked posts: a footnote warning label (on the left) and the blur filter covering the image or video content of the post (on the right).

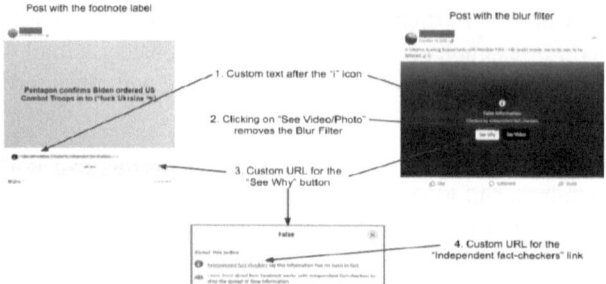

Fig. 1. Custom Features in ModSimulator.

Stimuli. After consenting to the research and completing screening questions, participants began interacting with posts in the Facebook-like simulation interface. Specifically, participants were invited to review and interact with 50 pre-selected posts about recent[1] events in Ukraine. The posts were displayed as search results that a typical Facebook user would see when searching for "Ukraine" on Facebook. The sample included a mix of the following posts: 35 posts (70%) in the sample came from credible news sources; 10 posts (20%) were opinions about politics and international relations of the U.S., Canada, NATO, EU, China, Ukraine, and Russia that cannot be fact-checked due to their subjective nature; and, 5 posts (10%) contained claims that have been fact-checked as "False". Our stimuli (i.e., the five claims rated as false, with or without a soft moderation intervention) were randomly placed throughout the simulated feed. Table A.2 lists the five false claims and representative posts selected for this study.

Soft Moderation Interventions. To test participants' propensity to engage with misinformation, participants were randomly assigned to one of the three conditions (~500 participants per condition). The three conditions displayed in Fig. 2 are as follows: 1) a control condition in which participants were exposed to misinformation (i.e., claims that have been rated as false by independent fact-checkers) without any soft moderation intervention, 2) an intervention showing the "False Information" label that the information is false in a footnote, and 3) an intervention using the blur filter and the "False Information" label covering the content.

Fig. 2. Three Study Conditions.

---

[1] "Recent" at the time of data collection in March 2023.

Research Question 1. We used the one-way ANOVA test to examine differences in engagement with misinformation across the three conditions. Content with higher levels of engagement is more likely to be viewed by a larger audience and is more likely to be promoted by social media algorithms. As a result, for this study, we are using engagement as the dependent variable, operationalized as counts for the various types of interactions with false claims, such as the number of shares and reactions (e.g., 👍Like, ♡Love, 😮Wow). For instance, an engagement score of 5 means there were 5 distinct interactions with posts featuring false claims. Since the purpose of this variable was to capture the potential level of support for claims that have been independently fact-checked and deemed false, we excluded counts of comments and the ' 😆Haha' reactions from the total number of interactions. This is because most comments left by the participants were sarcastic or aimed at refuting a particular claim. The same rationale was applied when excluding 'Haha' reactions from the overall engagement count.

Research Question 2. After participants spent at least 10 min interacting with the simulated Facebook-like interface, we asked them to complete post-intervention and demographic questions. The survey instrument is available in Appendix B. These questions helped us answer RQ2 by testing the potential relationship between the following user-specific factors and the likelihood of participants engaging with posts rated as 'False' by fact-checkers.

Trust in Institutions. We asked participants to rate their trust in news sources (mainstream news and partisan sites), different governments (Russia, Ukraine, U.S., and Canada), and fact-checking organizations. Following a previously validated scale [36], trust was measured from 1 ('None at all') to 5 ('A great deal'). Related to news consumption, we also included a question about the frequency of accessing news about the Russia-Ukraine war from various sources (print, radio, TV, online, and social media), ranging from 1 ('Never') to 5 ('Always').

Political Ideology and Populism. We measured participants' political leanings towards liberal or conservative ideology using Pew's Ideological Consistency Scale [48], adapted to the Canadian context. We also used the Populist Attitudes Scale [49] to measure participants' attitudes towards populism (e.g., anti-elitism, people-centrism).

Active Social Media Use. We operationalized this factor in terms of the frequency of social media use and the level of engagement in online discussions. To assess usage frequency, we asked participants how often they visit Facebook. To assess the overall level of engagement on the platform, we asked how often they make original posts, comment on or like other users' posts (as opposed to just reading them). These questions used a time-frequency scale from 'Never' to 'Daily'.

Prior Beliefs/Beliefs in Pro-Kremlin Claims. To operationalize this factor, we asked participants to rate the accuracy of the five false-rated claims displayed in the Facebook-like simulation interface on a scale of -2 ('Not at all accurate') to 2 ('Very accurate'). We then combined the responses to calculate the average score representing the independent variable 'Beliefs in pro-Kremlin claims'. The Cronbach's Alpha across all five claims was 0.856 (based on the standardized items), indicating a "very good" internal consistency.

Demographic Variables. Age was recorded as a categorical variable (18–24, 25–34, etc.). For consistency with Facebook Ads audience estimates, the gender variable was recorded as binary by asking participants how they prefer to identify themselves (woman or man). Participants were invited to provide more detailed information about their gender identification later in the survey.

Finally, since the dependent variable was the number of interactions with false claims, we used the total number of interactions as a control variable to address the scenario in which an individual who frequently engages with posts in the simulated feed may unintentionally engage with posts containing misinformation.

Using SPSS (v.28.0.1.1), we performed Automatic Linear Modelling (ALM) based on the Best Subsets model selection method [50] to identify the predictors with the strongest effects on the number of interactions with false claims. We set the confidence interval to 95% and used Akaike's Information Criterion Corrected (AICC) to measure the quality of the model and guide the selection process. The advantage of using ALM over other regression models in SPSS is that it has several data preparation procedures for the identification of outliers and variable selection [51]. ALM assesses and merges categories for categorical variables to maximize the association between independent variables and the target variable. For example, the 'Condition/Group' variable initially had three possible values: '1 - no intervention', '2 - footnote warning label', and '3 - blur filter'. Because there was only a small or no difference in the impact of this variable on the target variable, ALM has transformed this independent categorical variable into binary with values of 0 (in case of no intervention) and 1 (when either of the two interventions was present). We used SPSS to confirm no auto-correlation or collinearity between independent variables.

For both tests (one-way ANOVA for RQ1 and ALM for RQ2), we excluded 302 responses from participants who had not interacted with any posts (whether they featured a false claim or not). This is because we could not reliably confirm whether these participants engaged with the simulated Facebook environment. The final dataset for statistical testing included responses and interactions from 1198 (out of 1500) participants who interacted with the simulated feed at least once.

5   Results and Discussion

5.1   Do Soft Moderation Interventions Commonly Used by Social Media Platforms Reduce Engagement with Misinformation? (RQ1)

Table A.3 shows the number of participants for each condition and the mean value of interactions with false claims, including the standard deviation and minimum and maximum values. On average, the control group interacted 0.9 times with false claims, 1.5 more than either of the two intervention groups (0.62 for the footnote warning label group and 0.60 for the blur filter group).

The one-way ANOVA test indicates a significant difference in means among groups (F(2, 1195) = 7.207, p < 0.001), with a small effect size (η^2 = .012) (Table A.4). Because there is a significant difference in variance across groups as per Levene's test (Table A.5), we validated our results based on the Welch test (Table A.6). The Welch test rejected the null hypothesis of equal population means (F(2,779.044) = 6.563, p = 0.001), which confirmed that the means are not equal over all groups, even when the homogeneity assumption is violated, as in our case. However, the Welch test alone does not indicate which groups differ based on the means. Thus, we also conducted a post hoc Games-Howell test (Table A.7). The test found a statistically significant difference in means between the control group and each intervention group, 0.282 (SE = 0.092, p = 0.006, 95% CI [0.07, 0.50]) and 0.299 (SE = 0.089, p = 0.002, 95% CI [0.09, 0.51]), respectively. The mean difference in the number of interactions with misinformation between the two intervention groups was not statistically significant (M = 0.018, SE = 0.082, p = 0.974, 95% CI [−0.17, 0.21]). In other words, both tested interventions reduced the mean number of interactions with misinformation, but there is no statistically significant difference between them.

5.2 What User-Specific Factors Can Predict Users' Engagement with Misinformation? (RQ2)

The ALM regression model shows an accuracy of 57.6%. Table A.8 lists the independent variables found to be statistically significant in predicting the dependent variable (i.e., the number of interactions with posts featuring false claims, excluding comments and 'Haha' reactions) while controlling for the rest. Because we used the Best Subsets selection method in ALM, only factors that improve the predictive power of the final model are included in the resulting table. Furthermore, we focus only on the statistically significant factors (at the 0.05 level), excluding the two non-statistically significant factors ('Frequency of getting news from the print sources' and 'Frequency of posting to Facebook').

Factors **positively** predicting the dependent variable (in order of importance) are the total number of interactions across all posts (INTERACTIONS_ALL, β = 0.077, SE = 0.002, t = 37.884, p < 0.00), the average belief score in the five false claims (BELIEF, β = 0.107, SE = 0.024, t = 4.385, p < 0.001), belonging to the control group (GROUP = 0, β = 0.192, SE = 0.050, t = 3.811, p < 0.001), and trust in partisan sites for news about the Russia-Ukraine war (TRUST_PARTISAN, β = 0.065, SE = 0.026, t = 2.474, p = 0.014):

- The total number of interactions across all posts was included to account for circumstances in which a participant is generally active and interacts with posts indiscriminately (whether these posts contain misinformation or not). As expected, participants more engaged with the simulated feed were also more likely to interact with false claims, regardless of whether an intervention was used.
- Another expected result is that users who are more likely to believe in false claims are also more likely to interact with posts featuring a version of these claims, regardless of whether an intervention was used. This finding points to a potential limitation of fact-checking interventions, which may not work for social media users with pre-existing beliefs in pro-Kremlin claims.

- In line with the RQ1 result, users are more likely to engage with false claims when no intervention is applied.
- Finally, trusting partisan sites for news about the Russia-Ukraine war is also associated with the user interacting with false claims. This finding is also expected as partisanship is the most agreed-upon determinant among misinformation experts in predicting belief in and misinformation sharing [52].

In contrast, two factors that **negatively** predict the dependent variable (in order of importance) are trust in fact-checkers (TRUST_FACTCHECK, $\beta = -0.079$, SE $= 0.025$, t $= -3.170$, p $= 0.002$) and frequency of commenting on other people's posts (COMMENT, $\beta = -0.077$, SE $= 0.024$, t $= -3.228$, p $= 0.001$):

- The more users reported trusting fact-checking organizations, the less likely they were to engage with false claims while controlling for all other factors, including intervention. This finding suggests that increasing trust in fact-checking organizations may reduce the impact of misinformation.
- The frequency of commenting on Facebook posts (based on self-reported data) is also inversely related to the number of observed interactions with misinformation. People who were less likely to comment on Facebook posts were more likely to interact with false claims in the experiment. While this finding may be counter-intuitive, [38] found a similar trend that at least a third of their study participants engaged with misinformation, likely to publicly "denounce" the content of the posts as false. Another study on COVID-19 misinformation [53] discovered that active commentators tended to pay more attention to the accuracy of posts to avoid "looking stupid".

Political ideology, populism, news consumption, frequency of liking on Facebook, trust in governments, and demographic variables were excluded from the final model by ALM, suggesting these factors lack predictive power on engagement with misinformation. Further research is required to explain this result.

6　Conclusions

In this paper, we used ModSimulator to create a social media interface that mimics the experience of using Facebook. Using this interactive interface, we tested two common soft moderation interventions – a footnote warning label or a blur filter – to study how users respond to misinformation labels on social media posts.

Responding to **RQ1**, we find that the tested interventions reduced engagement with misinformation about the Russia-Ukraine war among Canadian Facebook users. The more restrictive intervention of adding the blur filter in front of a fact-checked image or video did not produce a stronger response. This finding held even when accounting for user-specific factors, as summarized below.

Responding to **RQ2**, we find that irrespective of the intervention used, there are other predictors of engagement with misinformation. On the one hand, individuals' beliefs in pro-Kremlin claims and trust in partisan sites for news about the Russia-Ukraine war increased the likelihood of engagement with misinformation. On the other hand, trust in fact-checking organizations and being an active commenter on Facebook decreases the likelihood of engagement with the five false claims presented in the study. This shows that, in addition to using soft moderation interventions, other factors play a role in social media users' decisions to engage with misinformation and should not be overlooked.

For example, in light of our results, we could explore options to increase trust in credible fact-checking organizations that provide assessments subsequently used for warning labels. Similar to our findings, previous research demonstrated that fact-checkers perceived as more credible tend to be more effective [54]. To be perceived as trustworthy, [55] suggests that fact-checking organizations should emphasize their usefulness, engage actively on social media, consider the importance of emotional perceptions of distrust, maintain transparency in their processes, and foster collaborative relationships with users. [32] advises fact-checkers to communicate their motives and identities clearly and proactively in order to increase trust in their reviews. [56] finds that independent fact-checking organizations are more effective in societies with low trust in public broadcasters. These are all reasonable and intuitive suggestions but are unlikely to be easily achievable without investment in journalism.

Another challenge for fact-checking is the issue of scalability. To address this challenge, researchers and organizations have experimented with using AI-driven solutions [57] and crowdsourcing [58]. However, fact-check labels are perceived by users as more trustworthy when done by human fact-checkers [59]. Only in cases of partisan content was fact-checking done by an AI or user consensus (i.e., crowdsourcing) viewed as more credible than fact-checks produced by human experts, at least in the experimental setting [60]. This suggests that while there is a need to optimize and streamline the fact-checking process to improve scalability, it remains crucial to involve experts in the loop of this process to ensure the accuracy of automation and instill trust in fact-checking – a viewpoint shared by the fact-checkers community [61].

From a future research perspective, our results suggest that soft moderation interventions may not be as effective with individuals who have prior belief in misinformation. In such cases, instead of simply stating that a claim is false, [41] suggests offering corrective information coupled with facts in a way that is "internally consistent" with the recipient's beliefs. [41] gives an example of how misinformation about mask usage to prevent COVID-19 transmission could have been diminished if public health agencies had acknowledged that some initial guidance suggesting masks were not needed for personal use was due to limited knowledge of the virus's airborne transmission. Developing personalized corrective messaging is not a straightforward task, but it is a promising direction for future research on misinformation interventions. Furthermore, with new tools like ModSimulator, researchers can now develop and test their own interventions using an interactive environment that balances experimental control and generalizability close to real-world contexts - a significant limitation of prior studies on misinformation intervention.

Appendix A: Supplementary Materials

Table A.1. Facebook User Estimates in Canada

Variable	Facebook User Estimates			
	Min	Max	Average (%)	N = 1.5K
Total Estimate	18.9M	22.2M		
Gender				
Women	9.9M	11.6M	53.75%	806
Men	8.5M	10M	46.25%	694
Total Estimate (Gender)*	18.4M	21.6M		
Age group				
18–24	1,9M	2.2M	10.10%	151
25–34	4.4M	5.2M	23.64%	355
35–44	3.8M	4.4M	20.21%	303
45–54	3.1M	3.6M	16.51%	248
55 +	5.5M	6.5M	29.55%	443
Total Estimate (Age group)*	18.7M	21.9M		
Region				
Ontario	6.8M	7.9M	36.55%	549
Quebec	4.5M	5.3M	24.35%	365
Western (Alberta, British Columbia, Manitoba, and Saskatchewan)	5.8M	6.9M	31.55%	473
Atlantic (New Brunswick, Newfoundland and Labrador, Nova Scotia, and Prince Edward Island)	1.3M	1.6M	7.19%	108
Territories (Northwest Territories, Yukon and Nunavut)	0.651M	0.766M	0.35%	5
Total Estimate (Region)*	18.4651M	21.7766M		

*Note: The estimates of the total number of users may not match because some users might be missing certain demographic information.

Table A.2. Sample False Claims related to the Russia-Ukraine war

#	False Claims	Sample Posts
1	"U.S. combat troops have been deployed to Ukraine" Fact-check: https://www.usatoday.com/story/news/factcheck/2022/11/14/fact-check-us-military-personnel-ukraine-inspectors-security/8262293001/	ThePatriotOasis BREAKING: Biden calls for a national draft. Men and women are to be selected to fight in Ukraine. BIDEN: "The recommended way forward will be to invoke the Selective Service Act, as is my authority as president," THE REALITIES OF NUCLEAR WAR 0:00 / 0:43 0 Comments Like Comment Share
2	"The U.K. has suspended aid to Ukraine" Fact-check: https://fullfact.org/online/sunak-ukraine-financial-support/	Light Spark BREAKING: Britain suspends aid to Ukraine due to financial problems. Sunak says Britain's "severe economic crisis" can no longer support aid to Ukraine. Me: Why withdraw now that Ukraine s decimated? PLEASE LIKE THIS POST AND SHARE 0 Comments Like Comment Share
3	"Poland intends to annex part of Ukraine" Fact-check: https://leadstories.com/hoax-alert/2022/09/fact-check-this-video-does-not-prove-poland-taking-first-step-toward-turning-ukraine-into-polish-colony.html	TFI Global Poland takes the first step towards turning Ukraine into a Polish colony Volhynia 0:59 / 1:12 0 Comments Like Comment Share

(continued)

Table A.2. (*continued*)

#	False Claims	Sample Posts
4	"Ukrainian soldiers are under the influence of drugs to hold on to the front" Fact-check: https://www-tf1info-fr.translate.goog/internati onal/video-les-soldats-ukrainiens-combattent-ils-sous-l-effet-de-la-drogue-captagon-2246735.html	
5	"A flag given to U.S. House Congress by Ukrainian President Volodymyr Zelenskyy in December 2022 contained Nazi Symbolism" Fact-check: https://www.snopes.com/fact-check/zelensky-con gress-flag/	

Table A.3. Participant Distribution (N) across Conditions (1,2,3) and Descriptive Statistics for Interactions with False Claims

Condition	N	Mean	Std. Deviation	Std. Error	95% Confidence Interval for Mean		Min	Max
					Lower Bound	Upper Dound		
1	369	.90	1.334	.069	.76	1.04	0	7
2	406	.62	1.213	.060	.50	.74	0	10
3	423	.60	1.133	.055	.49	.71	0	5
Total	1198	.70	1.231	.036	.63	.77	0	10

Table A.4. One-way ANOVA

	Sum of Squares	df	Mean Square	F	Sig.
Between Groups	21.623	2	10.811	7.207	<.001
Within Groups	1792.595	1195	1.500		
Total	1814.218	1197			

Table A.5. Tests of Homogeneity of Variance

	Levene Statistic	df1	df2	Sig.
Based on Mean	3.411	2	1195	.033
Based on Median	7.207	2	1195	<.001
Based on Median and with adjusted df	7.207	2	1173.539	<.001
Based on trimmed Mean	5.474	2	1195	.004

Table A.6. Robust Tests of Equality of Means

	Statistic[a]	df1	df2	Sig.
Welch	6.563	2	779.044	.001

[a] Asymptotically F distributed

Table A.7. Games-Howell Test

(I) Group	(J) Group	Mean Difference (I–J)	Std. Error	Sig.	95% Confidence Interval	
					Lower Bound	Upper Bound
1	2	.282*	.092	.006	.07	.50
	3	.299*	.089	.002	.09	.51
2	1	−.282*	.092	.006	−.50	−.07
	3	.018	.082	.974	−.17	.21
3	1	−.299*	.089	.002	−.51	−.09
	2	−.018	.082	.974	−.21	.17

*The mean difference is significant at the 0.05 level.

Table A.8. ALM Regression Model

Model Term	Coefficient	Std. Error	T	Sig.	95% Confidence Interval		Importance
					Lower	Upper	
Intercept	0.877	0.380	2.308	0.021*	0.132	1.623	
INTERACTIONS_ALL The total number of interactions with any post	0.077	0.002	37.884	0.000*	0.073	0.081	0.957
BELIEF The average score for believing in Pro-Kremlin claims about the war in Ukraine	0.107	0.024	4.385	0.000*	0.059	0.155	0.013
GROUP = 0	0.192	0.050	3.811	0.000*	0.093	0.291	0.010
COMMENT Q: Thinking about your Facebook use overall, how often do you comment on other people's posts?	−0.077	0.024	−3.228	0.001*	−0.124	−0.030	0.007
TRUST_FACTCHECK Q: How much trust do you have in the accuracy of information provided by fact-checking organizations like AFP Canada when evaluating claims made online?	−0.079	0.025	−3.170	0.002*	−0.128	−0.030	0.007
TRUST_PARTISAN Q: How much do you trust the accuracy of news about the Russia-Ukraine War from partisan sites?	0.065	0.026	2.474	0.014*	0.014	0.117	0.004

(*continued*)

Table A.8. (*continued*)

Model Term	Coefficient	Std. Error	T	Sig.	95% Confidence Interval		Importance
					Lower	Upper	
NEWS_PRINT Q: How often do you get news about the Russia-Ukraine War from the print (newspapers, magazines)?	0.031	0.020	1.559	0.119	−0.008	0.070	0.002
POST Q: Thinking about your Facebook use overall, how often do you make original posts?	0.036	0.024	1.512	0.131	−0.011	0.082	0.002

*Significant at the 0.05 level.

Appendix B: Survey Instrument

What is your age group?

- 18–24
- 25–34
- 35–44
- 45–54
- 55+

For the purposes of this study, how would you like to be identified?

Note: This question uses binary gender terms for consistency with Facebook estimates; you will have a chance to provide more detailed information about your gender identification later in the survey.

- Woman
- Man

What is your highest level of education earned?

- Some school, no degree
- High school graduate
- Some college, no degree
- College diploma
- Bachelor's degree
- Master's degree
- Professional degree (J.D., M.D., D.O., etc.)
- Doctorate degree

How often do you visit Facebook?

- Never (I have never had a Facebook account)
- Never (I used to have a Facebook account, but I don't use it any more or I deactivated/deleted it)
- Less than monthly
- Monthly
- Weekly
- Daily

Thinking about your Facebook use overall, how often do you…?

- Make original posts (POST)
- Like or use another reaction on other people's posts (LIKE)
- Comment on other people's posts (COMMENT)

Answer options: Never; Less than monthly; Monthly; Weekly; Daily

The next section will ask you questions about how you get news related to the war between Russia and Ukraine.

Definitions:

- News = information about events and issues beyond just your friends and family;
- Mainstream media = mass media organizations that report on news that reflects widely held views;
- Partisan sites = websites run by individuals or groups that advocate strongly for a particular political party, cause or person.

How often do you get news about the Russia-Ukraine War from the following sources?

- Print (newspapers, magazines)
- Radio (broadcast, satellite)
- TV (broadcast, cable)
- Online (news website or mobile app)
- Social media platforms/messaging apps

Answer options: Never; Rarely; Sometimes; Often; Always

How much trust do you have in the accuracy of information provided by fact-checking organizations like AFP Canada when evaluating claims made online?

- None at all
- A little
- A moderate amount
- A lot
- A great deal

How much you trust the accuracy of news about the Russia-Ukraine War from:

- Mainstream Media
- Partisan sites
- Friends and family
- Political parties and leaders

- Canadian Public Officials/Government ministries & departments
- U.S. Public Officials/Government ministries & departments
- Ukrainian Public Officials/Government ministries & departments
- Russian Public Officials/Government ministries & departments

Answer options: None at all; A little; A moderate amount; A lot; A great deal
To the best of your knowledge, how accurate are the following claims:

- "U.S. combat troops have been deployed to Ukraine"
- "The U.K. has suspended aid to Ukraine"
- "Poland intends to annex part of Ukraine"
- "Ukrainian soldiers are under the influence of drugs to hold on to the front"
- "A flag given to U.S. House Congress by Ukrainian President Volodymyr Zelenskyy in December 2022 contained Nazi Symbolism"

Answer options: Not at all accurate; Not very accurate; Not sure; Somewhat accurate; Very accurate
When faced with what you think is misinformation about the Russia-Ukraine War on Facebook, how likely are you to do the following?

Note: Generally speaking, misinformation is an incorrect, misleading or unproven claim presented as fact.

- Mute, unfollow, or block an account for sharing misinformation
- Directly challenge an account that shared misinformation
- Report an account/post that shared misinformation to the social media site
- Report an account/post that shared misinformation to the media
- Report an account/post that shared misinformation to law enforcement
- Limit your overall use of social media/messaging app
- Consult other sources to verify the information

Answer options: Extremely Unlikely; Somewhat Unlikely; Neither Likely nor Unlikely; Somewhat Likely; Extremely Likely
Please indicate how much you agree with the following statements about politicians and elected officials:

- The politicians in the parliament need to follow the will of the people.
- The people, not the politicians, should make our most important policy decisions.
- The political differences between the people and the elite are larger than the differences among the people.
- I would rather be represented by an ordinary citizen than an experienced politician.
- Elected officials talk too much and take too little action.
- What people call "compromise" in politics is really just selling out on one's principles.
- The particular interests of the political class negatively affect the welfare of the people.
- Politicians always end up agreeing when it comes to protecting their privileges.

Answer options: Strongly Disagree; Somewhat Disagree; Neither Agree nor Disagree; Somewhat Agree; Strongly Agree
Please choose one statement from each of the ten pairs below that most closely aligns with your political and societal views. Keep in mind that you may not fully agree with either statement, but please select the one that is closest to your views.

Code (1)	Code (0)
Government is almost always wasteful and inefficient	Government often does a better job than people give it credit for
Government regulation of business usually does more harm than good	Government regulation of business is necessary to protect the public interest
Poor people today have it easy because they can get government benefits without doing anything in return	Poor people have hard lives because government benefits don't go far enough to help them live decently
The government today can't afford to do much more to help the needy	The government should do more to help needy Canadians, even if it means going deeper into debt
Indigenous and Black people who can't get ahead in this country are mostly responsible for their own condition	Discrimination is the main reason why many Indigenous and Black people can't get ahead these days
Immigrants today are a burden on our country because they take our jobs, housing and health care	Immigrants today strengthen our country because of their hard work and talents
The best way to ensure peace is through military strength	Good diplomacy is the best way to ensure peace
Most corporations make a fair and reasonable amount of profit	Business corporations make too much profit
Stricter environmental laws and regulations cost too many jobs and hurt the economy	Stricter environmental laws and regulations are worth the cost
Homosexuality should be discouraged by society	Homosexuality should be accepted by society

References

1. Clayton, K., et al.: Real solutions for fake news? Measuring the effectiveness of general warnings and fact-check tags in reducing belief in false stories on social media. Polit. Behav. **42**, 1073–1095 (2020)
2. Gosnell, E., Berman, K., Juarez, L., Mathera, R.: How behavioral science reduced the spread of misinformation on TikTok (2021)
3. Papakyriakopoulos, O., Goodman, E.: The impact of twitter labels on misinformation spread and user engagement: lessons from trump's election tweets. In: Proceedings of the ACM Web Conference 2022, pp. 2541–2551. Association for Computing Machinery, New York (2022)
4. Pennycook, G., Bear, A., Collins, E.T., Rand, D.G.: The implied truth effect: attaching warnings to a subset of fake news headlines increases perceived accuracy of headlines without warnings. Manage. Sci. **66**, 4944–4957 (2020)
5. Aslett, K., Guess, A.M., Bonneau, R., Nagler, J., Tucker, J.A.: News credibility labels have limited average effects on news diet quality and fail to reduce misperceptions. Sci. Adv. **8**, eabl3844 (2022)
6. Badrinathan, S.: Educative Interventions to Combat Misinformation: Evidence from a Field Experiment in India. American Political Science Review (2021)

7. Guess, A.M., et al.: A digital media literacy intervention increases discernment between mainstream and false news in the United States and India. Proc. Natl. Acad. Sci. U.S.A. **117**, 15536–15545 (2020)
8. Pluviano, S., Watt, C., Della Sala, S.: Misinformation lingers in memory: failure of three pro-vaccination strategies. PLoS ONE **12** (2017)
9. Paul, C., Matthews, M.: The Russian "Firehose of Falsehood" Propaganda Model: Why It Might Work and Options to Counter It. Rand Corporation (2016)
10. Gigitashvili, G., Osadchuk, R.: How ten false flag narratives were promoted by pro-Kremlin Media. https://medium.com/dfrlab/how-ten-false-flag-narratives-were-promoted-by-pro-kremlin-media-c67e786c6085. Accessed 23 Sept 2022
11. Grossman, S., et al.: Full-Spectrum Pro-Kremlin Online Propaganda about Ukraine. https://fsi.stanford.edu/news/full-spectrum-propaganda-ukraine. Accessed 12 Sept 2022
12. Gruzd, A., Mai, P., Soares, F.B., Saiphoo, A.: The Reach of Russian Propaganda & Disinformation in Canada. Toronto Metropolitan University, Toronto (2022)
13. Silverman, C., Kao, J.: Infamous Russian Troll Farm Appears to Be Source of Anti-Ukraine Propaganda (2022). https://www.propublica.org/article/infamous-russian-troll-farm-appears-to-be-source-of-anti-ukraine-propaganda
14. Freelon, D., Wells, C.: Disinformation as political communication. Null. **37**, 145–156 (2020)
15. Ziemer, C.-T., Rothmund, T.: Psychological underpinnings of disinformation countermeasures: a systematic scoping review. (2022). https://doi.org/10.31234/osf.io/scq5v
16. van Stekelenburg, A., Schaap, G., Veling, H., Buijzen, M.: Investigating and improving the accuracy of US citizens' beliefs about the COVID-19 pandemic: longitudinal survey study. J. Med. Internet Res. **23**, e24069 (2021)
17. Ecker, U.K.H., Sharkey, C.X.M., Swire-Thompson, B.: Correcting vaccine misinformation: a failure to replicate familiarity or fear-driven backfire effects. PLoS ONE **18**, e0281140 (2023)
18. Basol, M., Roozenbeek, J., Berriche, M., Uenal, F., McClanahan, W.P., van der Linden, S.: Towards psychological herd immunity: Cross-cultural evidence for two prebunking interventions against COVID-19 misinformation. Big Data Soc. **8**, 20539517211013868 (2021)
19. Ma, J., Chen, Y., Zhu, H., Gan, Y.: Fighting COVID-19 misinformation through an online game based on the inoculation theory: analyzing the mediating effects of perceived threat and persuasion knowledge. Int. J. Environ. Res. Public Health **20**, 980 (2023)
20. Appel, R.E., et al.: Psychological inoculation improves resilience to and reduces willingness to share vaccine misinformatio (2024). https://doi.org/10.31234/osf.io/ek5pu
21. Jolley, D., Douglas, K.M.: Prevention is better than cure: addressing anti-vaccine conspiracy theories. J. Appl. Soc. Psychol. **47**, 459–469 (2017)
22. Reavis, R.D., Ebbs, J.B., Onunkwo, A.K., Sage, L.M.: A self-affirmation exercise does not improve intentions to vaccinate among parents with negative vaccine attitudes (and may decrease intentions to vaccinate). PLoS ONE **12**, e0181368 (2017)
23. Nyhan, B., Reifler, J.: The roles of information deficits and identity threat in the prevalence of misperceptions. J. Election. Publ. Opin. Parties **29**, 222–244 (2019)
24. Pennycook, G., Epstein, Z., Mosleh, M., Arechar, A.A., Eckles, D., Rand, D.G.: Shifting attention to accuracy can reduce misinformation online. Nature **592**, 590–595 (2021)
25. Sharevski, F., Alsaadi, R., Jachim, P., Pieroni, E.: Misinformation warning labels: twitter's soft moderation effects on COVID-19 vaccine belief echoes. arXiv preprint arXiv:2104.00779 [cs] (2021)
26. Sanderson, Z., Brown, M.A., Bonneau, R., Nagler, J., Tucker, J.A.: Twitter Flagged Donald Trump's Tweets With Election Misinformation: They Continued to Spread Both on and Off the Platform. Harvard Kennedy School Misinformation Review (2021)
27. Bhattacherjee, A., Sanford, C.: The intention–behaviour gap in technology usage: the moderating role of attitude strength. Behav. Inf. Technol. **28**, 389–401 (2009)

28. Mai, P., Gruzd, A.: The State of Social Media in Canada 2022. Toronto Metropolitan University (2022)

29. Newman, N., Fletcher, R., Robertson, C.T., Eddy, K., Nielsen, R.K.: Reuters Institute Digital News Report 2022. University of Oxford, Oxford (2022)

30. Enders, A.M., et al.: The Relationship Between Social Media Use and Beliefs in Conspiracy Theories and Misinformation. Political Behavior (2021)

31. Hutchens, M.J., Hmielowski, J.D., Beam, M.A., Romanova, E.: Trust over use: examining the roles of media use and media trust on misperceptions in the 2016 US Presidential election. Null. **24**, 701–724 (2021)

32. Primig, F.: The influence of media trust and normative role expectations on the credibility of fact checkers. Journalism Pract. 1–21 (2022)

33. Righetti, N.: Four years of fake news: a quantitative analysis of the scientific literature. First Monday **26** (2021)

34. Valenzuela, S., Halpern, D., Araneda, F.: A downward spiral? A panel study of misinformation and media trust in Chile. Int. J. Press/Polit. **27**, 353–373 (2022)

35. Rossini, P., Mont'Alverne, C., Kalogeropoulos, A.: Explaining beliefs in electoral misinformation in the 2022 Brazilian election: the role of ideology, political trust, social media, and messaging apps. Harvard Kennedy School (HKS) Misinformation Rev. **4** (2023)

36. Soares, F.B., Gruzd, A., Mai, P.: Falling for Russian propaganda: understanding the factors that contribute to belief in pro-Kremlin disinformation on Social Media. Soc. Media Soc. **9**, 20563051231220330 (2023)

37. Ecker, U.K.H., et al.: The psychological drivers of misinformation belief and its resistance to correction. Nat. Rev. Psychol. **1**, 13–29 (2022)

38. Carson, A., Gravelle, T.B., Phillips, J.B., Meese, J., Ruppanner, L.: Do brands matter? Understanding public trust in third-party Factcheckers of misinformation and disinformation on Facebook. Int. J. Commun. **17**, 25 (2023)

39. Calvillo, D.P., Ross, B.J.R., Garcia, R.J.B., Smelter, T.J., Rutchick, A.M.: Political ideology predicts perceptions of the threat of COVID-19 (and susceptibility to fake news about it). Soc. Psychol. Personal. Sci. **11**, 1119–1128 (2020)

40. Stecula, D.A., Pickup, M.: How populism and conservative media fuel conspiracy beliefs about COVID-19 and what it means for COVID-19 behaviors. Res. Polit. **8** (2021)

41. Johar, G.V.: Untangling the web of misinformation and false beliefs. J. Consum. Psychol. **32**, 374–383 (2022)

42. Aghajari, Z., Baumer, E.P.S., DiFranzo, D.: Reviewing interventions to address misinformation: the need to expand our vision beyond an individualistic focus. Proc. ACM Hum.-Comput. Interact. **7**, 87:1–87:34 (2023)

43. Gong, C., Ren, Y.: PTSD, FOMO and fake news beliefs: a cross-sectional study of Wenchuan earthquake survivors. BMC Publ. Health **23**, 2213 (2023)

44. Grinberg, N., Joseph, K., Friedland, L., Swire-Thompson, B., Lazer, D.: Fake news on Twitter during the 2016 U.S. presidential election. Science **363**, 374–378 (2019). https://doi.org/10.1126/science.aau2706

45. Knuutila, A., Neudert, L.-M., Howard, P.N.: Who is afraid of fake news? Modeling risk perceptions of misinformation in 142 countries. Harvard Kennedy School Misinf. Rev. (2022). https://doi.org/10.37016/mr-2020-97

46. [Removed for blind review]

47. Jagayat, A., Boparai, G., Pun, C., Choma, B.L.: Mock Social Media Website Tool (2021). https://docs.studysocial.media/

48. Dimock, M., Kiley, J., Keeter, S., Doherty, C.: Political Polarization in the American Public. Pew Research Center (2014)

49. Van Hauwaert, S.M., Schimpf, C.H., Azevedo, F.: The measurement of populist attitudes: testing cross-national scales using item response theory. Politics **40**, 3–21 (2020)

50. Brooks, G.P., Ruengvirayudh, P.: Best-subset selection criteria for multiple linear regression. Gen. Linear Model J. (2016)
51. Yang, H.: The Case for Being Automatic: Introducing the Automatic Linear Modeling (LINEAR) Procedure in SPSS Statistics, vol. 39 (2013)
52. Altay, S., Berriche, M., Heuer, H., Farkas, J., Rathje, S.: A survey of expert views on misinformation: definitions, determinants, solutions, and future of the field. Harvard Kennedy School Misinf. Rev. (2023)
53. Schuetz, S.W., Sykes, T.A., Venkatesh, V.: Combating COVID-19 fake news on social media through fact checking: antecedents and consequences. Eur. J. Inf. Syst. **30**, 376–388 (2021)
54. Liu, X., Qi, L., Wang, L., Metzger, M.J.: Checking the fact-checkers: the role of source type, perceived credibility, and individual differences in fact-checking effectiveness. Commun. Res. 00936502231206419 (2023)
55. Brandtzaeg, P.B., Følstad, A.: Trust and distrust in online fact-checking services. Commun. ACM **60**, 65–71 (2017)
56. Van Erkel, P.F.A., et al.: When are fact-checks effective? An experimental study on the inclusion of the misinformation source and the source of fact-checks in 16 European Countries. Mass Commun. Soc. 1–26 (2024)
57. Lim, G., Perrault, S.T.: XAI in Automated Fact-Checking? The Benefits Are Modest and There's No One-Explanation-Fits-All (2023). http://arxiv.org/abs/2308.03372
58. Allen, J., Arechar, A.A., Pennycook, G., Rand, D.G.: Scaling up fact-checking using the wisdom of crowds. Sci. Adv. **7**, eabf4393 (2021)
59. Seo, H., Xiong, A., Lee, D.: Trust it or not: effects of machine-learning warnings in helping individuals mitigate misinformation. In: Proceedings of the 10th ACM Conference on Web Science, pp. 265–274. Association for Computing Machinery, New York (2019)
60. Moon, W.-K., Chung, M., Jones-Jang, S.M.: How can we fight partisan biases in the COVID-19 pandemic? AI source labels on fact-checking messages reduce motivated reasoning. Mass Commun. Soc. **26**, 646–670 (2023)
61. Micallef, N., Armacost, V., Memon, N., Patil, S.: True or false: studying the work practices of professional fact-checkers. Proc. ACM Hum.-Comput. Interact. **6**, 1–44 (2022)

Crowdsourcing Statement Classification to Enhance Information Quality Prediction

Jaspreet Singh[1], Michael Soprano[2], Kevin Roitero[2],
and Davide Ceolin[3(✉)]

[1] Vrije Universiteit Amsterdam, Amsterdam, The Netherlands
[2] University of Udine, Udine, Italy
{michael.soprano,kevin.roitero}@uniud.it
[3] Centrum Wiskunde & Informatica (CWI), Amsterdam, The Netherlands
davide.ceolin@cwi.nl

Abstract. This paper explores the use of crowdsourcing to classify statement types in film reviews to assess their information quality. Employing the Argument Type Identification Procedure which uses the Periodic Table of Arguments to categorize arguments, the study aims to connect statement types to the overall argument strength and information reliability. Focusing on non-expert annotators in a crowdsourcing environment, the research assesses their reliability based on various factors including language proficiency and annotation experience. Results indicate the importance of careful annotator selection and training to achieve high inter-annotator agreement and highlight challenges in crowdsourcing statement classification for information quality assessment.

Keywords: Crowdsourcing Annotation · Information Quality Assessment · Argument Type Identification

1 Introduction

Misinformation significantly impacts society, making argument-checking a critical approach to combat this issue by assessing the quality of information beyond simple fact-checking [28]. This method leverages argument theory, which explores how arguments support or undermine each other through claims and premises within structured models [19]. However, the manual extraction and analysis of these argument structures are complex and time-consuming, leading to increased popularity in automated argument mining [12]. Identifying and classifying argument types in texts helps evaluate argumentative discourse, facilitated by the Argument Type Identification Procedure (ATIP) which uses the Periodic Table of Arguments (PTA) for classifying arguments [26,27]. This classification is crucial for understanding the arguments' strengths and identifying potentially misleading content.

In this paper, we explore the use of crowdsourcing [10] to identify statement types within texts and investigate how these types correlate with the quality of

M. Preuss et al. (Eds.): MISDOOM 2024, LNCS 15175, pp. 70–85, 2024.
https://doi.org/10.1007/978-3-031-71210-4_5

the items they describe. Specifically, we define argument types based on their relationships within texts. Our use case regards the analysis of movie reviews for two reasons: (1) movie reviews are semi-structured (composed of a structured rating and an unstructured text) and are then particularly convenient to analyze and provide initial insights that can be later adapted to unstructured items, and (2) movie reviews can be a vehicle of misinformation, especially when the movies analyzed have a significant social or cultural impact. This said, we focus on the possibility of employing crowd workers to identify argument building blocks, so our primary research question is: what are the reliability indicators of lay annotators of statement types? To address this, we undertake two main tasks: identifying reliable annotators and determining characteristics that correlate with their annotation performance. Features such as the annotators' language proficiency and their familiarity with annotation tasks are examined, providing insights into factors that may enhance the effectiveness of crowdsourcing in future studies.

The rest of the paper continues as follows. Section 2 introduces related work. Sections 3 and 4 describe the methodology and the dataset considered. Section 5 presents the results obtained, then discussed in Sect. 6. Section 7 concludes.

2   Related Work

Previous studies have investigated text argument annotation through crowdsourcing to maximize the inter-annotator agreement (IAA). For example, Jiang et al. [11] have focused on developing a workflow in which non-expert annotators can filter the set of options to choose for annotation and indicate that they are unsure instead of selecting an answer. Experts evaluated annotations above a certain level of inter-annotator disagreement. Even though this approach addresses uncertainty to enhance the reliability of annotated data, it does not completely take on the challenge of improving the reliability of annotated data. Miller et al. [17] developed a method to be applied by untrained annotators. By setting up a crowdsourcing task, annotations have been collected and the reliability of the annotations has been established by comparing them to expert-trained annotations. In this line of research, a study similar to the present work was done by Li et al. [14] who explored argument structures in Chinese hotel reviews using crowdsourcing. Past research has mainly focused on gathering reliable data to train a model with a high accuracy [1,2,8,10,15,21]. However, we focus on creating accurate data for analysis rather than building an accurate model. Methods used to obtain accurate data by minimizing expert annotations have been introduced in previous studies [11,17], but while they focus on arguments, we focus on their building blocks, i.e., statement types.

3   Methodology

The development of automated argument mining tools involves several steps. First, data acquisition involves gathering a dataset containing texts rich in arguments for crowdsourcing. Following this, the task design and execution phase

Table 1. Quality dimensions according to which film reviews are evaluated.

Quality dimension	Explanation
Accuracy	Provides a measurement of the overall truthfulness of the review
Precision	Indicates whether the film review is precise or vague
Completeness	Indicates whether the film review is complete
Neutrality	Measures the objectiveness of the film review
Comprehensibility	Measures the understandability and readability of the review
Trustworthiness	Measures the overall trustworthiness of the film review

involves setting up a crowdsourcing task to collect human-provided annotations of the argument types found in these texts.

In the final phase (data analysis and evaluation), we analyze the annotated data to assess the agreement among the annotators and the consistency of the results. We identify reliable annotators by selecting and analyzing the features of the annotators providing the most reliable annotations.

Crowdsourcing Task Description. The crowdsourcing task for this project is structured as follows. We implemented it using the Crowd_Frame framework [24] and published it on Amazon Mechanical Turk. Participants are first presented with a task description, which outlines the nature of the task, the data that will be collected, its intended use, and detailed instructions for completing the task. Then, participants fill in a questionnaire to collect demographic and professional information, including the participant's age, highest level of education, continent of residence, industry of employment, native languages, familiarity with film reviews, and experience with data annotation. Lastly, participants proceed to the film review annotation and assessment phase. Here, each crowd worker is presented with a single film review. The task involves evaluating the review concerning specific quality dimensions (similar to [3,25]) and annotating the review by highlighting statements and classifying them into one of three types: Statement of Fact, which is verifiable through empirical observation; Statement of Value, which expresses an evaluative judgment; and Statement of Policy, which recommends a course of action.

4 Data

The first step of our method regards the collection from Rotten Tomatoes of a dataset of film reviews to be annotated by crowd workers. To collect film reviews, a selection of five films, including Split (2016), Get Out (2017), Bird Box (2018), Parasite (2019), and Smile (2022),[1] has been made and twenty reviews of each

---

[1] See, for instance, www.rottentomatoes.com/m/split_2017.

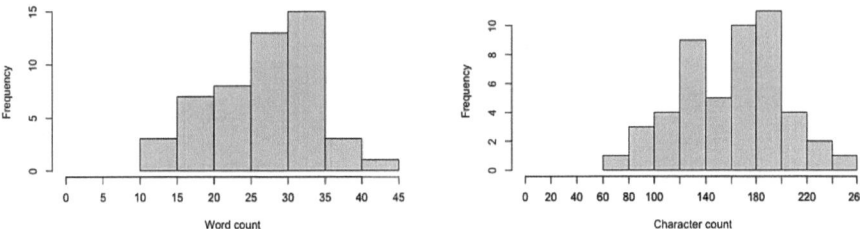

Fig. 1. Histograms visualizing the distribution of word (left plot) and character (right plot) count in the fifty film reviews.

film have been collected (one hundred in total). Selecting a review requires evaluating whether it is to the point, ensuring its text is adequately long and contains actual arguments justifying why the particular film is considered good or bad. Therefore, reviews that are too short and do not contain relevant arguments have not been selected as well as relatively long reviews, because those would increase the complexity of the task significantly. We selected fifty reviews out of the hundred collected. The selected reviews are approximately equal in length to corroborate fairness toward crowd workers who assess and annotate the reviews. The average word count of the reviews is 27.78 with the shortest review containing twelve words and the longest one 41 words. Figure 1 (left plot) presents the distribution of the word count of the reviews. The average number of characters is 160.48 with the shortest review consisting of 78 characters and the longest of 245 characters. Figure 1 (right plot) shows the distribution of the review lengths in terms of character count. Also, two one-, two-, three-, four- and five-star reviews have been selected for each of the five films to ensure that the distribution of the ratings is uniform among each of the films. The resulting dataset consists of the film name, the reviewer id, and text, rating (on a scale of 1–5 stars), and timestamp for each review. Each crowd worker annotates and evaluates ten reviews. Similarly to the setting of Iskender et al. [10], each review is annotated by five crowd workers. We recruited 25 crowd workers and each crowd worker is assigned ten random reviews.

5 Results

5.1 Identification of Reliable Annotators

The first part of the analysis is concerned with the identification of reliable annotators. The most reliable annotators are those whose IAA is above a certain threshold. To determine the IAA, we used a custom metric. First, we calculate the IAA and investigate low-performing annotators. This is important because a low IAA can be due to: (1) the annotator performed poorly because they were solely focused on the reward (2) the task might have been stated in a complex manner; and (3) the reviews were difficult to annotate.

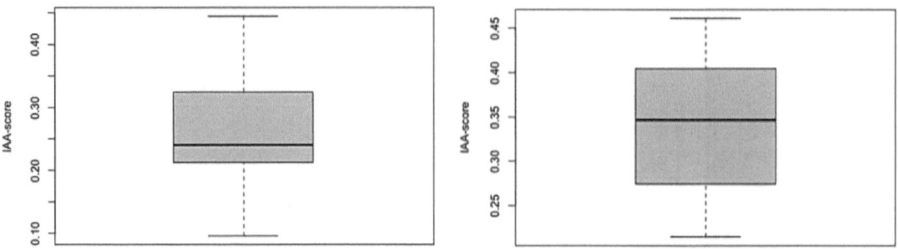

Fig. 2. Boxplot of the individual IAA scores of the whole 25 annotators (left plot) and of the 18 less reliable annotators (right plot), where the IAA score is calculated by taking the average of every pair-wise IAA score between two annotators whose sets of annotated reviews overlap.

Inter-annotator Agreement. Calculating the IAA for the obtained data requires a custom quality measure because data consists of free-text annotations. IAA measures the extent to which annotators agree on assigning labels to instances from a particular category. This can give insights into the clarity of the annotation guidelines, the degree of consistency in understanding among the annotators, and the reproducibility of the annotation task [6]. IAA can also be used to measure the reliability of the annotations. The IAA for data obtained from categorical and ordinal labeling tasks can be measured using, for example, Scott's π [23], Cohen's κ [4] and Fleiss' κ [7]. Due to the complex nature of the task, an IAA measure that takes the arbitrary number of annotated text spans per review into account must be considered. To this end, Hripcak and Rothschild [9] investigated the exact and relaxed span agreement. The former evaluates whether two annotations have the same text span boundaries and are labeled with the same category, and the latter can be divided into two categories, namely one-sided boundary agreement and token overlap agreement. To measure agreement between two annotators, A and B, F1-scores have been calculated by considering annotations provided by A as gold standard annotations and annotations provided by B as predicted annotations and vice versa. An F-measure that does not take negative case counts must be considered because negative case counts cannot be determined in the current study. Therefore, the method for calculating F-scores presented by Lee and Sun [13] has been adopted in combination with text span agreement. Two annotators agree on a statement if there is at least one matching token and if the argument labels match. The IAA between two annotators A and B is measured using an F1-score. We calculated the IAA score between every possible pair of annotators who annotated the same review. Hereafter, the sum of the calculated IAA scores has been divided by the number of IAA scores, which resulted in an average IAA score of 0.258. The average number of annotations provided per annotator is roughly 25. Figure 2 (left plot) provides a boxplot of the individual IAA scores. The individual IAA score for each annotator is calculated by taking the average of all IAA scores between the annotator and every other annotator if their annotated reviews overlap.

Identification of Unreliable Annotators. There are seven annotators whose individual IAA scores are within the lower whisker of the boxplot. Five out of these seven annotators provided one annotation per review, consisting of an arbitrary word, and the other two provided 62 and hundred annotations, respectively, consisting of, an arbitrary word and arbitrary text span. Without taking these seven annotators in consideration, the resulting average IAA score equals 0.283. The corresponding boxplot can be found in Fig. 2 (right plot). Henceforth, the remaining eighteen annotators will be taken into consideration for the analysis.

Whereas the average number of annotations provided per annotator was 25 before removing the seven annotators, it is now roughly 28. From the remaining eighteen annotators, five annotators have an individual IAA score within the range of the lower whisker of the boxplot. These five annotators provided on average 37 annotations, which is somewhat large compared with the average of number annotations per annotator. It must be pointed out that most of the annotations provided by three out of these five annotators are arbitrary text spans or single-word annotations. In particular, these three annotators have an average of 41 annotations per annotator. This results, on its turn, in a large number of FNs or FPs and yields low IAA scores. The other two annotators, A and B, seem to have provided decent annotations and a decent number of annotations, namely 30 and 33, respectively. However, when calculating pair-wise IAA scores between two annotators, many IAA scores are zero for both these annotators in comparison with the other annotators. It might be the case that the reviews assigned to these two annotators were relatively difficult to annotate compared to the other reviews. We look at the quality scores of these reviews to investigate this claim. In particular, the precision and comprehensibility scores will be analyzed. The comprehensibility indicates how well the review is understandable and readable, which is related to its precision score, which expresses whether the use of language is precise [18]. The average scores for each quality dimension, mentioned in Table 1, for each review, are calculated by taking the sum of the scores assigned to the review by five annotators and dividing it by five. Then, six boxplots, one for each quality dimension are created. See Fig. 2 (Fig. 3).

We checked if the reviews assigned to annotators A and B have low-quality scores compared to other reviews, i.e., whether their scores fall within the lower whisker of a boxplot. The counts of low scores among reviews annotated by A, B, and overall are presented in Table 2. Specifically, we report the precision and comprehensibility scores in Table 3. Annotators A and B commonly annotated one review and nine mutually exclusive reviews. Table 2 shows the count of low-quality dimension scores among the reviews annotated by annotators A, B, and overall. Most reviews assigned to annotators A and B, namely 8 and 7, have at least one low-quality dimension score (see Table 2). Table 3 specifically presents the count of reviews with low precision or low comprehensibility scores. As shown in Table 3, it can be seen that roughly half of the reviews with a low precision score have been assigned to both annotators A and B, namely four to annotator A and three to annotator B. This is also the case for the reviews with a low comprehensibility score, where ten out of the total 21 reviews with a low

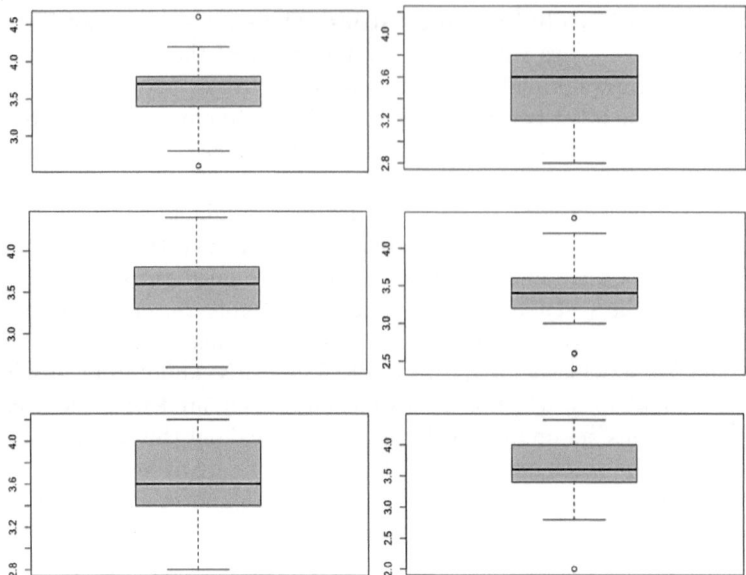

Fig. 3. Boxplots of the scores of the fifty reviews for each quality dimension. From the top left corner, left to right: Accuracy, Precision, Completeness, Neutrality, Comprehensibility, Truthfulness.

comprehensibility score have been assigned to both annotators A and B. It must be stated that the review commonly annotated by annotators A and B has a low comprehensibility score. At least half of the reviews assigned to annotators A and B have a low comprehensibility score. Another interesting finding is that five out of the seven reviews with low precision and comprehensibility scores have been assigned to annotators A and B, of which three to annotator A and two to annotator B. To check the significance of these findings, low precision, and comprehensibility scores among the reviews assigned to the other annotators have also been counted. However, we found no significant difference between the low score counts of reviews assigned to annotators A and B and the other annotators. No conclusion regarding the association between the difficulty of interpreting the reviews assigned to annotators A and B based on the quality scores of their reviews and the performance of the annotators can be drawn due to the limited availability of data.

Correlation Between Individual and Average Item IAA Scores. The correlation between the individual IAA scores and the average IAA scores of the annotated film reviews of the eighteen annotators has been examined. This required calculating an IAA score for each film review based on the annotations provided by the five annotators assigned to that film review, which has been determined as follows. A score has been calculated for every character in the film review by taking the number of annotators, based on the majority of the

Table 2. Counts of the reviews with one or more low-quality scores, i.e., those within the lower whisker of any of the boxplots shown in Fig. 2.

	Ann. A	Ann. B	Overall
#Reviews with 1 low quality dimension score	2	2	11
#Reviews with 2 low quality dimension scores	2	3	10
#Reviews with 3 low quality dimension scores	1	0	3
#Reviews with 4 low quality dimension scores	0	3	4
#Reviews with 5 low quality dimension scores	2	0	3
#Reviews with 6 low quality dimension scores	1	0	1
#Reviews with at least 1 low quality dim. score	8	7	32

Table 3. Counts of the reviews that have low precision and comprehensibility scores, where a low precision or comprehensibility score falls within the lower whiskers of the corresponding boxplots shown in Fig. 2.

	Ann. A	Ann. B	Overall
#Reviews with low precision score	4	3	16
#Reviews with low comprehensibility score	6	5	21
#Reviews with low precision and compr. scores	3	2	7

annotators, whose annotated text spans contained or did not contain that character, and dividing it by five. The sum of these scores is then divided by the number of characters in the film review, resulting in an average item IAA score. To calculate the average item IAA score for every annotator, the sum of the item IAA scores of the ten film reviews annotated by that annotator is divided by ten. The resulting average and individual IAA scores are presented in Table 4.

To observe whether there is a correlation between the individual IAA scores and the average item IAA scores, Spearman's correlation ρ, Kendall's correlation τ, and Pearson's correlation coefficient have been calculated. The resulting coefficients are, respectively, $\rho = 0.111$ with a p-value $= 0.662$, $\tau = 0.060$ with a p-value $= 0.732$ and $r = -0.034$ with a p-value $= 0.892$, suggesting there is no relationship between the individual IAA scores and the average item IAA scores. This implies that the performance of the annotators was necessarily dependent on the difficulty of the film reviews assigned to them. Next to the average item IAA score, the average quality scores for each of the six quality dimensions, namely accuracy, precision, completeness, neutrality, comprehensibility, and trustworthiness, have been calculated for each of the eighteen annotators. This has been done by taking the sum of the average quality scores of the ten film reviews assigned to an annotator for a given quality dimension and dividing it by ten. The resulting average quality scores have been set out in Table 5.

Table 4. Individual and average item IAA scores of the annotators.

Annotator	Individual IAA score	Average item IAA score
C	0.302	0.716
D	0.402	0.736
E	0.316	0.707
F	0.406	0.733
G	0.406	0.689
H	0.406	0.728
I	0.358	0.706
J	0.336	0.748
K	0.397	0.643
L	0.296	0.751
M	0.423	0.702
N	0.461	0.730
O	0.400	0.720
P	0.269	0.718
Q	0.215	0.710
R	0.251	0.713
S	0.275	0.710
T	0.255	0.701

The correlation between the individual IAA scores and averages of the six quality dimensions, presented in Table 5, have been calculated and summarized in Table 6. Interpretations of Spearman's ρ, Kendall's τ, and Pearson's correlation coefficient have been adopted from Dancey and Reidy [5], Schober et al. [22] and Ratner [20], respectively. The correlation between the individual IAA scores and the average precision scores seems negligible, considering the given values for Spearman's ρ and Kendall's τ. This might imply that the film review being written in a precise or vague manner does not affect the performance of the annotator. There is a moderate relationship between the IAA scores and the average accuracy, average completeness, average neutrality, and average trustworthiness scores according to Kendall's τ and Pearson's correlation coefficients. Since accuracy relates to the truthfulness of a film review, a positive correlation between the performance in terms of IAA scores and the average accuracy score would be expected. Truthful statements are more likely to be annotated than false statements by annotators. There seems to be a moderate correlation between the performance and the average completeness scores, which can be because completeness indicates how many arguments are contained in a film review. A positive moderate correlation between the performance and the average neutrality scores indicates that a film review written objectively is easier to annotate. It might be easier to correctly label objective statements. There is also

Table 5. Average quality scores for each of the eighteen annotators

Annotator	Avg. accuracy	Avg. precision	Avg. completeness	Avg. neutrality	Avg. comprehensibility	Avg. trustworthiness
C	3.56	3.56	3.44	3.40	3.58	3.84
D	3.62	3.72	3.66	3.54	3.92	3.94
E	3.64	3.52	3.56	3.24	3.56	3.56
F	4.16	3.40	3.64	3.52	3.80	3.80
G	3.64	3.40	3.56	3.30	3.44	3.66
H	3.72	3.70	3.66	3.46	3.70	3.74
I	3.42	3.46	3.48	3.18	3.56	3.54
J	3.44	3.62	3.40	3.44	3.70	3.68
K	3.48	3.74	3.70	3.48	3.78	3.78
L	3.60	3.56	3.24	3.42	3.68	3.64
M	3.76	3.52	3.54	3.52	3.62	3.58
N	3.66	3.72	3.70	3.62	3.74	3.80
O	3.62	3.62	3.60	3.46	3.54	3.64
P	3.60	3.46	3.40	3.38	3.48	3.52
Q	3.64	3.52	3.48	3.40	3.46	3.68
R	3.68	3.78	3.64	3.50	3.80	3.58
S	3.52	3.60	3.46	3.48	3.50	3.54
T	3.38	3.56	3.56	3.26	3.52	3.54

a moderate correlation between the IAA scores and the average comprehensibility scores when taking Spearman's ρ and Pearson's correlation coefficients. A positive moderate correlation between the IAA scores and the average comprehensibility scores might be because a film review with a higher comprehensibility score is easier to understand and read by an annotator.

Selection of the Most Reliable Annotators. It is important to consider an objective criterion to obtain accurate data and an adequate sample size to select reliable annotators. Cohen's κ between 0.21 and 0.40 suggest fair agreement among annotators [16]. Applying a threshold of 0.40 to select annotators results in seven annotators. Using a stricter threshold by selecting annotators whose IAA scores are in the upper whisker of the boxplot depicted in Fig. 2, i.e. between 0.405 and 0.461, yields a set of annotators containing five annotators (see Table 7). The number of annotations decreases by 15% selecting a threshold of 0.405 instead of 0.400, which is 1.25% higher. So, we select a threshold of 0.400.

Table 6. Spearman's ρ, Kendall's τ, and Pearson's coefficients to determine the correlation between individual IAA scores and the quality dimensions.

Quality dimension	ρ	τ	r
Accuracy	0.452	0.329	0.345
Precision	0.001	0.020	0.109
Completeness	0.518	0.352	0.549
Neutrality	0.464	0.334	0.392
Comprehensibility	0.367	0.287	0.417
Trustworthiness	0.475	0.331	0.489

Table 7. Number of annotators along with the total number and percentage of annotations based on two thresholds for the individual IAA score.

Threshold	#annotators	#annotations	% annotations
0.400	7	147	29.3%
0.405	5	125	24.9%

Main Findings Related to the Identification of Reliable Annotators. The main results concerning identifying reliable annotators have been summarized as follows. (1) The initial set of 25 annotators has an average IAA score of 0.258 with the average number of annotations provided per annotator being 25. (2) The average item IAA score for each of the 18 annotators with lower reliability is 0.715. (3) The Spearman's correlation ρ, Kendall's correlation τ, and Pearson's correlation coefficients are $\rho = 0.111$, $\tau = 0.060$ and $r = -0.034$, indicating no relationship between the individual and the average item IAA scores. (4) Spearman's correlation ρ, Kendall's correlation τ, and Pearson's correlation coefficients suggest that the relationship between the individual IAA scores and the average accuracy scores is negligible, but the correlation between the individual IAA scores and the average precision, completeness, neutrality, comprehensibility, and trustworthiness scores is moderate.

5.2   Features of Reliable Annotators

In the second part of the analysis, an effort has been made to investigate whether we can extract features that the most reliable annotators have in common. The answers to the questions relating to language fluency, familiarity with film reviews, and familiarity with data annotation contained in the questionnaire are utilized as features. The total number of annotators considered equals eighteen of which seven annotators are considered the most reliable. We found that all of the most reliable annotators are native English speakers, whereas 89% of all annotators are native English speakers. Since the task has been formulated in English, it might be beneficial to employ native English speakers or annotators whose proficiency in English equals that of a native English speaker. Regarding language proficiency, respectively, 71% of the most reliable annotators are proficient in two or more languages, which is the case for 61% of all annotators.

We found that roughly half of the most reliable annotators rarely read film reviews, while roughly one-third of all annotators rarely read reviews. The majority of the most reliable annotators who read film reviews more frequently read them regularly or very often. When considering all annotators, however, roughly one-third of them sometimes read film reviews and roughly one-third read film reviews regularly or very often. Regarding the familiarity with writing film reviews among the most reliable annotators, we found that 25% have never written a film review, while the rest have written some film reviews. We also found that 22% of all annotators have never written a film review, the majority have written some reviews and 6% have written a fair number of reviews. It seems that a greater proportion of all annotators is more familiar with reading and writing film reviews compared to only the most reliable annotators. By contrast, a greater proportion of the most reliable annotators, namely roughly 72%, is fairly familiar with data annotation compared to all annotators of which 56% are fairly familiar with data annotation and of which 11% are somewhat familiar data annotation. Roughly 29% of the most reliable annotators indicated that the crowdsourcing task introduced in the current work is their first data annotation task, while this was the case for 33% of all annotators. Since the annotation task in the present study regards film reviews, it might also be advantageous to consider solely those annotators who read or write film reviews regularly.

Summary of the Main Findings Concerning the Most Reliable Annotators

- The most reliable annotators are native English speakers (89% overall).
- 71% and 61% of the most reliable annotators and all annotators, respectively, are proficient in two or more languages.
- 43%, 14%, and 43% of the most reliable annotators rarely, sometimes, and frequently read reviews; these proportions are valid overall.
- 25% most reliable annotators are familiar with writing reviews; most have written some film reviews. Overall, 22% have never written a film review, and again most have written film reviews.
- 72% most reliable annotators are fairly familiar with data annotation, whereas the rest are not. Overall, 56% are fairly familiar, 11% are somewhat familiar and 33% are not familiar with data annotation.

6   Discussion

The current paper aims to research how to extract features of reliable lay annotators of film review annotations. As a result, the analysis consists of two parts: identifying reliable annotators and extracting their possible features. The first part of the analysis has been performed in four steps, including calculating the

IAA scores, identifying unreliable annotators, calculating correlations between the IAA scores, and selecting the most reliable annotators. The first step resulted in 25 IAA scores with an average of 0.258. Seven annotators have been removed from the set of annotators in the second step because they provided arbitrary annotations. The resulting set contains eighteen annotators with an average IAA score of 0.283. The correlation between the IAA scores, the average item IAA scores and the average quality dimension scores of the annotated film reviews has been computed for each of the eighteen annotators in the third step. No correlation has been found between the IAA scores and the average item IAA scores, meaning that the difficulty of the film reviews assigned to an annotator does not affect their performance. Concerning the IAA scores and average quality dimension scores, positive moderate correlations between the IAA scores of the annotators and the average accuracy, completeness, neutrality, comprehensibility, and trustworthiness scores have been found. There is, however, no correlation between the performance in terms of IAA scores and the average precision scores. We then selected the most reliable annotators based on a threshold. The threshold of 0.400, suggesting fair agreement [16], has been applied. This results in a set of seven annotators with 147 annotations, which is 29.3% of all annotations. Increasing the threshold by choosing the value of 0.405, which includes all scores in the upper whisker of the boxplot of the IAA scores, yields a set of five annotators with 125 annotations, i.e., 24.9% of all annotations. Increasing the threshold by 1.25%, from 0.400 to 0.405, results in a decrease in the number of annotations by 15%, thus a threshold of 0.400 has been chosen. Hereafter, the analysis proceeds with the second part, where we seek features of the most reliable annotators. Even though there are some interesting findings about the features of all annotators, including the most reliable annotators, it is not possible to distinguish reliable annotators from the rest of the annotators based on the given features, including whether an annotator is a native English speaker, the number of proficient languages, familiarity with reading or writing film reviews and familiarity regarding data annotation tasks.

7   Conclusion

We employed 25 annotators, only 7 of whom are classified as reliable. This poses a challenge for feature extraction because of the trade-off between accuracy and size, which could be solved only by recruiting more annotators. This paper collected features that might have been useful for the identification and future employment of crowd workers on MTurk for annotating film reviews. Future work on analyzing annotations obtained from different platforms is suggested. Also, there is abundant room for further progress in identifying reliable annotators, although this requires using different text types and collecting more features.

Eighteen annotators are not classified as reliable. Next to the individual IAA score, an average item IAA score for each annotator has been calculated. The average item score of an annotator depends on the item scores given to the ten film reviews assigned to the annotator, where an item score is computed based on the agreement of the five annotators that annotated the item. The purpose of calculating average item IAA scores is to examine whether there is a correlation between those scores and the individual IAA scores. If there is a correlation between the individual IAA scores and the average item IAA scores, it would mean that the annotators' performance depends on the difficulty of the film reviews assigned to them, which should not be the case ideally. Another factor that requires consideration is the quality of the text to be annotated, which might also affect the annotators' performance. The correlation between the review quality in terms of accuracy, precision, completeness, neutrality, comprehensibility, and trustworthiness scores and the individual IAA scores has been surveyed. The findings suggest a correlation between the accuracy, completeness, neutrality, and comprehensibility scores, and the individual IAA scores. Ideally, the quality dimension scores should be uniform among all reviews. Besides data on the difficulty and quality of the film reviews, it would be valuable to obtain expert annotations. This would have allowed the validation of the computed IAA scores besides a more reliable selection of annotators. This among other recommendations has been summarized in the following guidelines for future research. (1) A sufficient number of annotators is of crucial importance to be able to retain a sufficient number of reliable annotators. (2) It is advised to ensure that the items that will be annotated are uniform in every possible aspect to prevent the annotator's performance from being dependent on the item's quality. (3) In addition to collecting annotations, it is helpful to collect data to assess the difficulty and quality of the annotated items to assess whether the difficulty or quality affected the performance of the annotators. (4) When possible, collect expert annotations to filter out unreliable annotators and identify reliable annotators.

Acknowledgements. This research is supported by the Netherlands eScience Center project "The Eye of the Beholder" (project nr. 027.020.G15), and it is part of the AI, Media & Democracy Lab (Dutch Research Council project number: NWA.1332.20.009). For more information about the lab and its further activities, visit https://www. aim4dem.nl/.

This research is also supported by the European Union's NextGenerationEU PNRR M4.C2.1.1 – PRIN 2022 project "20227F2ZN3 MoT–The Measure of Truth: An Evaluation-Centered Machine-Human Hybrid Framework for Assessing Information Truthfulness" (20227F2ZN3_001, CUP G53D23002800006), and by the Strategic Plan of the University of Udine–Interdepartmental Project on Artificial Intelligence (2020–2025).

References

1. Addawood, A., Bashir, M.: "What is your evidence?" A study of controversial topics on social media. In: ArgMining2016, pp. 1–11. ACL, August 2016
2. Bosc, T., Cabrio, E., Villata, S.: DART: a dataset of arguments and their relations on Twitter. In: LREC, pp. 1258–1263. ACL (2016)
3. Ceolin, D., Primiero, G., Soprano, M., Wielemaker, J.: Transparent assessment of information quality of online reviews using formal argumentation theory. Inf. Syst. **110**, 102107 (2022)

4. Cohen, J.: A coefficient of agreement for nominal scales. Educ. Psychol. Measur. **20**, 37–46 (1960)

5. Dancey, C.P., Reidy, J.: Statistics Without Maths for Psychology: Using SPSS for Windows. Prentice-Hall Inc., USA (2004)

6. Feier, A.: Reach consensus faster by using IAA charts in the annotation lab. https://www.johnsnowlabs.com/reach-consensus-faster-by-using-iaa-charts-in-the-annotation-lab/. Accessed 03 Apr 2023

7. Fleiss, J.L.: Measuring nominal scale agreement among many raters. Psychol. Bull. **76**, 378–382 (1971)

8. Goudas, T., Louizos, C., Petasis, G., Karkaletsis, V.: Argument extraction from news, blogs, and social media. In: Likas, A., Blekas, K., Kalles, D. (eds.) SETN 2014. LNCS (LNAI), vol. 8445, pp. 287–299. Springer, Cham (2014). https://doi.org/10.1007/978-3-319-07064-3_23

9. Hripcsak, G., Rothschild, A.S.: Agreement, the F-measure, and reliability in information retrieval. J. Am. Med. Inf. Ass. **12**, 296–298 (2005)

10. Iskender, N., Schaefer, R., Polzehl, T., Möller, S.: Argument mining in tweets: comparing crowd and expert annotations for automated claim and evidence detection. In: Métais, E., Meziane, F., Horacek, H., Kapetanios, E. (eds.) NLDB 2021. LNCS, vol. 12801, pp. 275–288. Springer, Cham (2021). https://doi.org/10.1007/978-3-030-80599-9_25

11. Jiang, Y., Zhu, H., Kummerfeld, J.K., Li, Y., Lasecki, W.: A novel workflow for accurately and efficiently crowdsourcing predicate senses and argument labels. In: EMNLP, pp. 415–421. ACL, November 2020

12. Lawrence, J., Reed, C.: Argument mining: a survey. Comput. Linguist. **45**(4), 765–818 (2019)

13. Lee, G.E., Sun, A.: A study on agreement in PICO span annotations. In: Proceedings of the 42nd International ACM SIGIR Conference, pp. 1149–1152. ACM (2019)

14. Li, M., Geng, S., Gao, Y., Peng, S., Liu, H., Wang, H.: Crowdsourcing argumentation structures in Chinese hotel reviews. In: SMC, pp. 87–92. IEEE (2017)

15. Lindahl, A.: Annotating argumentation in Swedish social media. In: ArgMining Workshop, pp. 100–105. ACL, December 2020

16. McHugh, M.L.: Interrater reliability: the kappa statistic. Biochemia Medica **22**, 276–282 (2012)

17. Miller, T., Sukhareva, M., Gurevych, I.: A streamlined method for sourcing discourse-level argumentation annotations from the crowd. In: NAACL, pp. 1790–1796. ACL, June 2019

18. Nordquist, R.: Definition and examples of vagueness in language. https://www.thoughtco.com/vagueness-language-1692483. Accessed 25 Sept 2023

19. Plug, H., Wagemans, J.: Argument-checken als een methode voor het identificeren van desinformatie. In: Proceedings of VIOT2024. University of Twente (2024)

20. Ratner, B.: The correlation coefficient: Its values range between +1/-1 or do they? J. Targ. Measur. Anal. Market. **17**(2), 139–142 (2009)

21. Schaefer, R., Stede, M.: Annotation and detection of arguments in tweets. In: Proceedings of the 7th Workshop on Argument Mining, pp. 53–58. ACL, December 2020

22. Schober, P., Boer, C., Schwarte, L.A.: Correlation coefficients: appropriate use and interpretation. Anesth. Analg. **126**(5) (2018)

23. Scott, W.A.: Reliability of content analysis: the case of nominal scale coding. Public Opin. Q. **19**(3), 321–325 (1955)

24. Soprano, M., Roitero, K., Bombassei De Bona, F., Mizzaro, S.: Crowd_frame: a simple and complete framework to deploy complex crowdsourcing tasks off-the-shelf. In: WSDM 2022, pp. 1605–1608. ACM (2022)
25. Soprano, M., et al.: The many dimensions of truthfulness: crowdsourcing misinformation assessments on a multidimensional scale. IP&M **58**(6), 102710 (2021)
26. Wagemans, J.: Constructing a periodic table of arguments. In: Argumentation, Objectivity, and Bias: Proceedings of the 11th International Conference of the OSSA, pp. 1–12, May 2016
27. Wagemans, J.H.M.: Argument Type Identification Procedure (ATIP) - Version 4. https://periodic-table-of-arguments.org/argument-type-identification-procedure. Accessed 21 Mar 2022
28. World Health Organization: Infodemic. https://www.who.int/health-topics/infodemic/understanding-the-infodemic-and-misinformation-in-the-fight-against-covid-19. Accessed 29 Apr 2024

The Spread of Anti-vaccination Memes on Facebook

Aleksi Knuutila[1]([⊠]), Anna George[2], Jonathan Bright[3], Kate Joynes-Burgess[4], and Philip Howard[2]

[1] University of Helsinki, Unioninkatu 35, 00170 Helsinki, Finland
`aleksi.knuutila@helsinki.fi`
[2] Oxford Internet Institute, 1 St Giles', Oxford OX1 3JS, UK
[3] Turing Institute, 96 Euston Road, London NW1 2DB, UK
[4] Oxford Internet Institute, University of Oxford, Oxford, UK

Abstract. False claims about vaccines can find large audiences online, leading to vaccine hesitancy. The most influential content on social media is often visual, but studies about misinformation largely focus on text instead of images. This study uses new image analysis capabilities that Facebook and Instagram have made available to understand the spread of visual anti-vaccination memes on these platforms. We identified 200 influential memes that contain scepticism or hesitancy towards vaccines and the 15,000 public Facebook accounts on which the memes have been shared. We describe the memes' spread on a large scale by identifying communities of accounts and describing the diffusion pathways of memes between the communities. We develop a novel method of testing whether a meme has spread from one community of accounts to another that works on sequential time series alone. We identify 16 distinct communities of Facebook accounts and categories them based on thematic and regional focus. Anti-vaccination memes originate predominantly from North American Facebook accounts. These accounts often focus on opposing COVID-19 policies or promoting conspiracy theories about elites. Memes from these communities also spread internationally, particularly to Europe, demonstrating their influence beyond North America. The analysis demonstrates that memes receive the most engagement within their initial community. However, their overall reach depends on their ability to spread to other communities. This suggests that the ability of memes to find large audiences is based on their capacity to spread beyond their original contexts and to be used by groups with potentially different agendas.

Keywords: Anti-vaccine activism · memes · Facebook · network structures · information diffusion

1 Introduction

Over the past decade, anti-vaccination rhetoric has become part of the mainstream discourse regarding the public health practice of childhood vaccination [6]. Its proponents utilise social media to foster online spaces that strengthen and popularise anti-vaccination

The original version of the chapter has been revised. A missing author's name has been added. A correction to this chapter can be found at
https://doi.org/10.1007/978-3-031-71210-4_9

M. Preuss et al. (Eds.): MISDOOM 2024, LNCS 15175, pp. 86–100, 2024.
https://doi.org/10.1007/978-3-031-71210-4_6

discourses [12]. One influential form of media in these communities is memes - static images, typically with some text layered on top, which can be used to communicate simple, persuasive concepts. Memes can have a significant impact because they often gather large audiences, communicate simple, powerful messages and elicit strong emotional reactions. They are simple visual forms of communication which can potentially "go viral" and spread beyond the original communities of interest they were created in.

Describing the spread of memes is particularly difficult as they are often copied from one place and posted to another without any attribution, obscuring their origin and the steps they take moving from one place to another. Hence, it has been difficult to scientifically study memes' origin and propagation patterns on a large scale. Visual material on the Internet in general been studied much less than textual forms of information [11]. In contemporary debates about vaccinations, when new types of claims and evidence are emerging all the time, visual and memetic forms of communication deserve particular attention.

We use time series data about posts containing anti-vaccination memes to answer the following questions:

- What communities do anti-vaccination memes transmit through?
- How important is the crossing from one community to another for the visibility of anti-vaccination memes?

One challenge in studying memes is that there is often a lack of meta-data about the source of the content. In our paper, we use timestamp information and time series analyses to detect when the meme first appeared on the platform and how it spread through the platform. This approach allows us to map the large-scale patterns of diffusion of anti-vaccination memes, from American conservative accounts to European and African groups, in a statistically robust and interpretable form.

2   Related Work

Visual media have distinct advantages over text. Images and image-text combinations offer what Shifman calls "high information density" [16], i.e. messages in this form can be understood at a glance. Images can elicit strong emotional reactions in people, especially if they display something graphic, such as the use of violence. Memes have frequently been used to refer to particular kinds of images, though the concept more broadly encompasses all cultural artefacts. In an influential article on the concept, Wiggins and Bowers offer a broader definition of a meme, seeing it as "remixed or parodied spreadable media" [20]. The term "spreadable media" points to the capacity of contemporary digital media to spread quickly and gather large audiences when large numbers of people share it on their networks. Spreadable media would include, for instance, YouTube videos, which can be viewed millions or even billions of times through the sharing of links. The type of meme shared on social media at a given time can correspond to life events or current internet culture 'fads'. What is specific to memes is the remixes or alterations that the media undergo when they spread. It can be difficult to find the "original authors" of memes as each person can alter the text or image of a meme and then spread their version to their network. However, the various versions of memes can still convey similar information or be related to a similar topic. This article focuses on visual still images (e.g., memes) with anti-vaccination content.

Social media exhibits the phenomenon of homophily, i.e. the fact that relationships form more likely between people who are similar in some sense [14]. An obvious example of this is that information tends to spread between accounts that share a common language or common interests. As a result, the network of accounts has a community structure, i.e. there are clusters of accounts that are more densely connected between themselves and have fewer connections with other accounts. This structure, in turn, affects the way information, including memes, travels through the network, for instance, by limiting the global flow of information since leaps between the communities are less likely [15].

Social media data has made it possible to model the effects of community structure on the flow of memes. Weng et al. [19], for instance, demonstrate that jumping between many communities early in a meme's life cycle predicts its future popularity. Several studies have also looked at the structure of specifically vaccination-related communities online. Studies on vaccination information overall on Twitter often find a single anti-vaccination community with little contact with pro-vaccination users [11]. Johnson et al. [9] find many distinct communities of anti-vaccination users on Facebook. They claim that the anti-vaccination communities are localised geographically, for instance, based on US states, but share information effectively through additional communities with a global orientation.

Memes have often been described as originating from relatively small communities of dedicated hobbyists before jumping to other demographics and large audiences. De Zeeuw et al. [4], for instance, discuss a diffusion pattern they name "normiefication", in which a cultural artefact from a fringe online subculture finds a larger and more dispersed audience, for instance, through going viral on Facebook or being replicated in newspapers or broadcast media. In this work, they found that platforms such as YouTube and Reddit were "bridge platforms", meaning they brought fringe ideas to the mainstream, including mainstream news media [4].

3 Methodology

3.1 Data Collection

This article uses data from CrowdTangle [2]. CrowdTangle is a service operated by Facebook that tracks Facebook, Instagram, and Reddit posts. This report uses data about text in images to search for memes. Since 2018, Facebook has done optical character recognition on a large scale on images shared on both Facebook and Instagram [17]. The platform uses optical character recognition to determine what text images contain and publishes this information as part of the image's metadata. CrowdTangle collects this information in its database and makes it possible to search for images based on the text contained therein. This makes it possible to find all posts containing particular memes in Crowdtangle's database by searching for distinctive phrases that are part of the memes. The CrowdTangle database contains public accounts on Instagram, pages, groups, and verified profiles on Facebook. For the sake of simplicity, we refer to pages, groups and profiles as "Facebook accounts" in this article. CrowdTangle's database is not comprehensive, but it contains almost all public Facebook pages and groups with more than 50,000 followers and a significant share of smaller accounts [3].

In the first step of the research, we identified 200 memes with anti-vaccination themes with a relatively large audience. We searched for images on Crowdtangle based on the text content in the images and limited the search to one year, from the 15th of February 2020 to the 15th of February 2021. Notably, this period is mostly focused on the time before actual vaccination programmes, which in Europe and the United States began in December 2020. The results, however, point to the fact that there was an active discussion of the vaccines even prior to the vaccination programmes. The keywords we used are "vaccination", "vaccinate", "vaccine", "pfizer", and "astrazeneca". For each day this year, we obtained 2,000 images that contained text that matched the keywords and had received an exceptional amount of engagement given the account they had been posted in (i.e., were "overperforming" in CrowdTangle's terminology). The results from these searches were aggregated by the image texts, i.e. we identified the text contents of images that occurred frequently in this dataset.

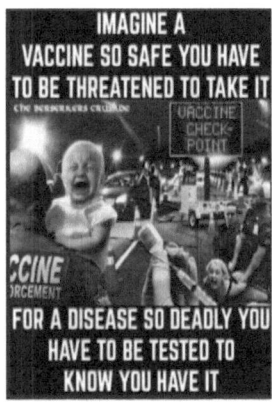 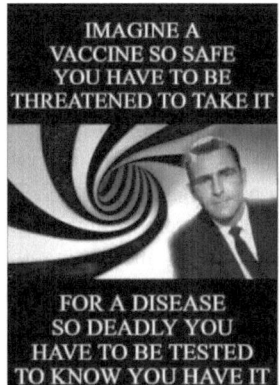 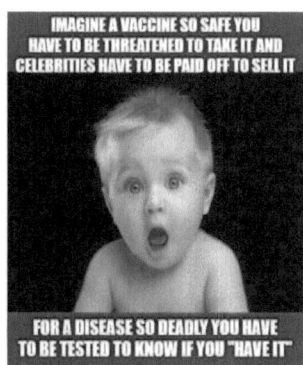

Fig. 1. An example of variations of an anti-vaccination meme in which the text content stays the same, but the visual template changes

We identify anti-vaccination memes from this dataset. We reviewed the most frequently reposted images and selected anti-vaccination memes with the following criteria:

- The images express opposition or scepticism towards vaccines, including but not limited to vaccines against the coronavirus.
- We include statements that vaccines are not necessary for the lack of harm from pathogens, the description of vaccination side effects, expressing hesitancy because of questionable motivations attributed to the government or pharmaceutical companies, or general negative statements related to the vaccine (such as "Down with vaccines").
- We also include humorous or satirical statements in this category when they imply a stance against vaccinations, even when this stance is not intended sincerely. This humour could take, for instance, the form of mocking public figures associated with vaccines, such as Fauci or Gates, for their work on the vaccine.
- We exclude images that are screenshots of social media posts or screenshots of news articles where these do not have any user-generated alterations made to them.

One research team member went through images in the Crowdtangle search results until 200 distinct anti-vaccination memes had been identified. This number of distinct memes was identified after examining 2065 images. The coding of this researcher was verified through double coding a sample of 100 decisions, with 50 of both images that had been coded as anti-vaccination memes and images that had not. The Cronbach's alpha indicator describing the reliability of the coding was 0.81, indicating good reliability in the coding.

For each anti-vaccination meme we identified, we made global searches on Crowd-Tangle based on the meme's text content. This allowed us to find all the copies of the same images shared on Facebook and variations of the same meme where the visual content had changed, but the text had remained the same. Figure 1 provides an example of variations in a meme where the text stays the same. In this example, all three images would have been grouped as instances of the same meme. Memes with the same image but different text would have been grouped as distinct memes.

3.2 Hierarchical Clustering of Accounts

The 200 anti-vaccination memes in our dataset have been shared in 14,594 Facebook accounts. Our analysis focuses not on individual accounts on Facebook but rather on what we call communities, i.e. groups of accounts that are densely connected in terms of frequently sharing posts from one account to another. The focus on communities will make large-scale diffusion patterns interpretable and provide insights that would be lost by focusing on, for instance, the individual most influential accounts.

Our community detection method is based on forming a graph in which the nodes are Facebook accounts, and the edges are formed based on posts being shared from one account to another. To create this graph, we do not use posts exclusively related to anti-vaccination memes but all posts shared between the accounts. This is because few memes shared between accounts have information about their origins, and using the full set of posts shared between accounts reflects the affinity between accounts better.

Some Facebook posts contain information about where the contents of the posts are shared from. The source of the post's content is recorded when people share it from one account to another using Facebook's internal sharing functionality (similar to retweets). Notably, this information about the source of shared information is not always available. For instance, for our dataset of anti-vaccination memes, information about the source of the posts was available 29% of the time. This metadata is insufficient for unbiased, reliable inference about the transmission of anti-vaccination memes specifically. However, the information about the source of posts is enough to understand the larger overall pattern of connections between accounts, at least when there are enough data points available.

We download up to 5,000 posts from each account from the previous 12 months to create the graph. From these posts, we identify shares of posts that had originated from other Facebook accounts. Based on such shares, we form a directed graph with weights reflecting the frequency of shares. The resulting graph contains 147,188 edges, an average of 10.0 edges for every account. We want to focus our analysis on accounts with a substantial number of connections to other accounts by taking the 10th k-core of this graph, i.e. focusing on the maximal subgraph that contains nodes with ten edges or more. This subgraph has 5,405 accounts with 115841 edges. We selected the 10th k-core because we estimate that for accounts with less than ten connections to other accounts, we cannot reliably estimate which community individual accounts should be connected to accounts with less than ten connections to other accounts. We chose ten as a relatively high and conservative threshold, given that there is some randomness and uncertainty about which post shares on Facebook contain the metadata about the source of the content.

We use Ward's method [13] to identify a hierarchy of potential communities. Ward's method is agglomerative, i.e. it starts from all observations forming separate communities and chooses which communities to merge at each step following an objective function. In our study, we create node embeddings based on generalised singular value decomposition embeddings at ten dimensions. We then apply Ward's minimum variance criterion as an objective function, i.e. merging communities at each step that increases the within-communities variance the least. The resulting hierarchy describes many different ways the data can be clustered and how individual communities can be broken up or combined depending on the desired level of resolution.

4 Identifying Transmission Patterns Without Metadata About Sources

As mentioned above, for a large share, the metadata about the source of their content is unavailable. To study the transmission of anti-vaccination memes from one community to another, we develop a method that does not rely on metadata about sources but works based on time series data describing when specific memes appeared in specific communities. We use time series data that describes the first appearance of every 200 memes within every community (if they appeared in the community at all). We estimate the spreading pattern by looking at whether memes appear systematically in one community before appearing in another. This pattern, a meme in one community systematically preceding another, does not prove an actual causal connection, as confounding factors might cause it. Nonetheless, it is a pattern that we would necessarily observe if memes spread from one community to another.

Our estimate of the spreading pattern is based on comparing observations to a null model. For the null model, we assume that the frequency of each meme posted to each community is the same as that observed, but the sequence of the postings is random. With statistical tests, we can derive the likelihood that the meme appears in one community before another for any meme and pair of communities.

In the null model, the likelihood that the meme will first appear in a particular community is:

$$p_{X,m} = \frac{N_{X,m}}{N_{all,m}}, \text{ where N is the number of memes } m \text{ in the community } X$$

The likelihood of a meme appearing in one community X it appears in community Y in the null model can be simplified to

$$p_{X,Y,m} = \frac{p_{X,m}}{p_{X,m} + p_{Y,m}}$$

The equations give us the expected frequency at which the meme appears in one community before another if the posts in one community do not influence other communities at all. We assess the likelihood that the distribution of the expected and observed frequencies is the same using the G-test or the log-likelihood ratio test [21]. This statistical test is performed for every pair of two distinct communities in a set of communities. This means that the number of statistical tests is high. To correct the so-called multiple testing problem, we apply the Benjamini-Hochberg procedure to adjust p-values [18]. The subsequent analysis discusses adjusted p-values.

4.1 Semi-supervised Selection of Communities

Above, we described the hierarchical community detection method, which results in a hierarchy that describes how individual communities can be combined or split apart. Based on the hierarchy, it is possible to choose many different sets of communities for analysis. For our analysis, we developed a novel approach for selecting sets of communities, applying the method of identifying transmission to the community hierarchy. We call this approach semi-supervised because it combines the results from the unsupervised hierarchical community detection we performed with Ward's method with the additional prior knowledge about potential communities, specifically the time series data about the appearance of anti-vaccination memes.

We search for the best selection of a set of communities, using the communities hierarchy from Ward's method as a set of options. Our evaluation of a particular selection of communities is based on the certainty with which we can trace the movement of memes from one community to another. We want to select sets of communities with explanatory power for describing the transmission of memes, i.e. sets of communities for which there is statistically significant transmission according to the methodology described above. Moreover, we aim to select sets of communities where as many as possible have both incoming and outgoing connections of transmission. This is done to identify rich and descriptive networks between communities. We hence divide every community's connections to other communities into incoming and outgoing connections. This difference is based on comparing observed data with the null model described above. Where a meme in a particular community precedes a meme appearing in another community at a frequency higher than expected by the null model, we classify the connection as an outgoing connection and vice versa.

We formalise this selection process with a cost function, to reward the selection of communities with both incoming and outgoing connections that are statistically significant. The cost function takes a sum of all p-values above the significance threshold and adds a constant alpha value for every p-value below the threshold. Alpha is a parameter that defines how much weight to give to significant connections relative to reducing the p-value of non-significant connections. For this work, we used an alpha value of -0.5.

We use the following cost function:

$$Cost = |S| \cdot \alpha + \sum_{p \in NS} p$$

where:

$$S = p \in P(I) \cup P(O) \,|\, p < \text{threshold}$$

and

$$NS = p \in P(I) \cup P(O) \,|\, p \geq \text{threshold}$$

Here, (I) and (O) represent the set of all incoming and outgoing connections where observed < expected and observed > expected, respectively. (P(I)) Moreover, (P(O)) represent the lowest p-value of these connections. (α) is the alpha value, (|S|) is the number of significant p-values.

Given this cost function, we search through the hierarchy of communities and identify the set of communities for which the cost function gives the lowest value. We start from the top of the hierarchy (with two communities containing all the accounts in the dataset) and recursively evaluate whether the selection is improved by replacing individual communities with their subcommunities in the community hierarchy. We run the beam search tree traversal algorithm to go through the options in the community hierarchy recursively [10]. For our study, we used a beam width of 3 and traversed 50,000 options for sets of communities.

The Girvan-Newman modularity score attained with Ward's method was 0.64. However, the resulting set of communities only has three statistically significant connections between the communities. This means that an unsupervised community detection method does not result in a choice of communities that can be used to explain the spreading of memes. In contrast, the semi-supervised method finds 19 statistically significant connections between the communities. The resulting set of communities has a Girvan-Newman modularity score of 0.54.

5 Results

5.1 Describing the Resulting Communities

The methodology we described resulted in 16 distinct communities, encompassing 5405 Facebook accounts. To describe the communities, we read through the list of 20 accounts that had shared the largest amount of anti-vaccination memes in each community. Additionally, we examined the most distinctive words in the names of accounts in each community according to the metric of Scaled F-Scores [7]. Two researchers worked on the interpretation to increase the validity of the community description.

The results are summarised in Table 1. For readability, we first categorised the regional focus of every community. The largest share of the communities were focused on the United States or Canada. Some of the communities also contained largely English-language accounts with an international focus, while some also had a range of African, Australian or European accounts. Moreover, we categorised the communities based on their thematic content. Many of the communities contained predominantly accounts focused on communicating and coordinating opposition to COVID-19 restrictions ("Re-Open California #EndTheLockdown") or discussing what we called elite conspiracies (e.g. "Exposing the Satanic World Government"). Many North American communities focused on supporting individual conservative politicians or parties, most prominently Donald Trump. Especially in Europe, we found many communities containing accounts of political extra-parliamentary protest movements, such as the Yellow Vests.

Table 1. 16 communities of Facebook accounts, with a classification of their regional focus and thematic focus, distinctive words in account names and descriptive statistics

Label	Region	Type	Distinctive uni/bi-grams in account names	# accounts	# posts with memes
A1	US/Canadian	Elite conspiracy		8	65
A2	US/Canadian	Anti-Covid policy	trudeau, canadian, alberta, masks, freedom fighters	261	1011
A3	US/Canadian	Anti-Covid policy	wrong, awaken, cosmic, save america, natural	178	594
A4	US/Canadian	Conservative politics	lake, unfiltered, angry, fake, politically incorrect	214	505
B1	International	Elite conspiracy	flat earth, exposing the, david icke, collective, elite	610	2309
B2	US/Canadian	Conservative politics	vote, trump train, deplorable, americans for, joe biden	921	2137
B3	US/Canadian	Conservative politics	wisconsin, excessive quarantine, against excessive, reopen, protect	122	300
B4	US/Canadian	Conservative politics	president trump, america great, protest, nevada, utah	479	1329
C1	International	Elite conspiracy	black lives, jamaica, positive, hip hop, conscious	396	882
C2	International	Elite conspiracy		37	126
C3	African	Cultural	anc, eff, zimbabwe, marcos, duterte	381	776
C4	African	Cultural	nigeria, zambia, biafra, malawi, university	741	1152

(*continued*)

Table 1. (*continued*)

Label	Region	Type	Distinctive uni/bi-grams in account names	# accounts	# posts with memes
C5	Australian	Conservative politics	aussie, australia, stand up for, stop the, sovereign	148	479
C6	American	Conservative politics	ted cruz, michigan, latinos, indiana, liberty memes	284	630
C7	European	Anti-systemic	gilets jaunes, vegan, romania, france, italia	396	702
C8	European	Anti-systemic	ireland, nederland, waarheid, tegen, yellow vest	229	556

We described such groups based on the concept of anti-systemic movements [8]. In particular, African communities contained a relatively wide variety of accounts that were not overtly political but focused on questions such as religion, parenting and nutrition. We categorised these accounts under the category "Cultural".

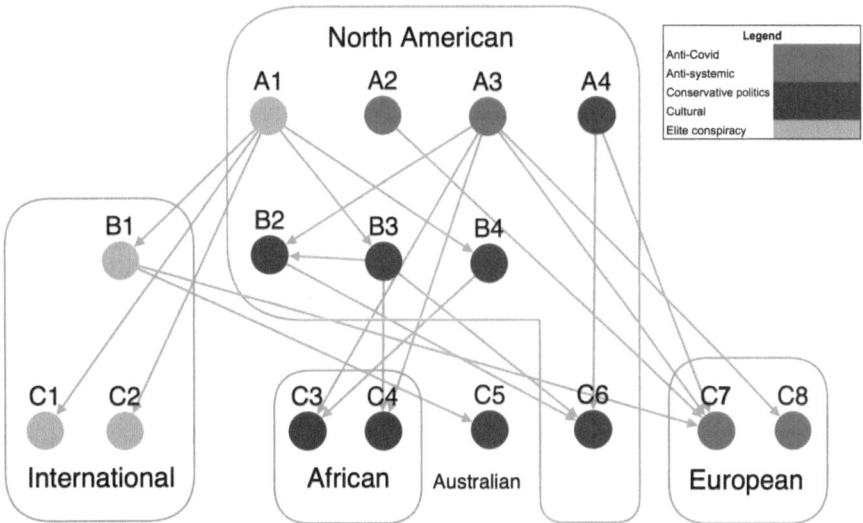

Fig. 2. A network graph displaying the detected movement of memes between communities of accounts, with the thematic and regional classification of the communities

5.2   The Spreading Pattern of Anti-vaccination Memes

Figure 2 shows a graph of connections between the communities, visualised using the Dagre layout [5]. We draw edges in the graph in all cases where there is a statistically significant connection between the communities, i.e. the test described above suggests that memes spread from one community to another. The significance test is based on aggregate data about all of the 200 anti-vaccination memes we identified. In this graph, the communities in the topmost row only have outgoing connections, the middle row has outgoing and incoming connections, and the bottom row has only incoming connections. We also labelled the communities to reflect their position in this network. Communities whose label starts with A are upstream in the network, i.e., they have outgoing edges online. In contrast, communities with the label B have both in-going and outgoing edges, and communities with the label C have only in-coming edges (i.e. they are downstream in the movement of memes).

Our results indicate that anti-vaccination memes originate from communities with predominantly North American accounts. The communities upstream from other communities include those focused on Anti-Covid policies (A2 and A3) and a community focused on elite conspiracies (A1). One upstream community (A4) was focused on conservative politics, but to a large extent, the conservative politics communities were further downstream. This suggests that the online spaces on Facebook where memes are first shared or where they are created are within accounts focused on opposing COVID-19 policies or those focused on a range of elite-related conspiracy theories. The presence of the A1 community in the graph suggests that very small communities (8 Facebook accounts in the case of A1) can have a large influence since this community has statistically significant connections to three other communities focused on elite conspiracies and two communities focused on conservative politics.

Figure 2 also describes a clear regional pattern. The memes in our study originate exclusively from groups associated with the United States and Canada. We identify some international, African, Australian and European communities that are further downstream. Connections with Europe and Africa illustrate that accounts that focus on American conservative politics and opposition to COVID-19 policies have influence and find an audience also outside of the region of North America. It is also notable that European communities have statistically significant connections with several different thematic types of communities. This suggests that there is no single pathway but multiple connections through which anti-vaccination memes spread to accounts in Europe.

5.3   The Impact of Spreading Between Communities

In this section, we describe how important it is for memes to cross boundaries for their lifecycle and popularity. In our dataset, memes traverse an average of 10.6 of the 16 communities, with a standard deviation of 3.3. Since our sampling strategy emphasised trending memes, many of them can be expected to move successfully between communities. It takes an average of 5.7 days for a meme to leave the first community in which it appears.

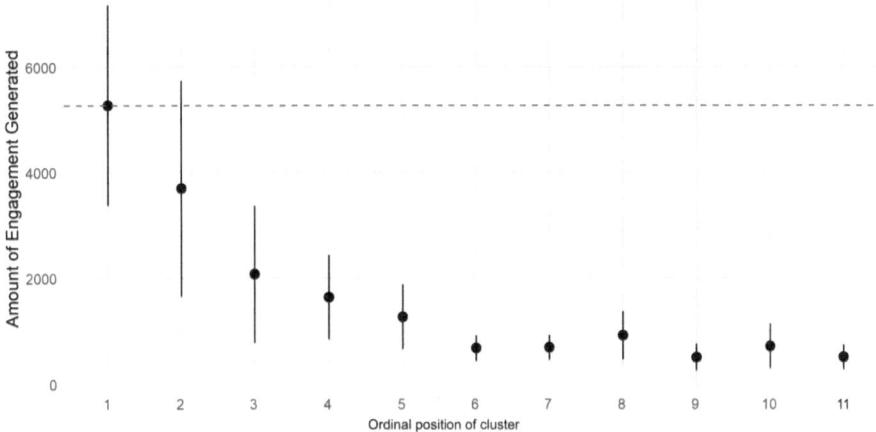

Fig. 3. The amount of engagement received by anti-vaccination memes in the first and subsequent communities in which they appeared

Figure 3 describes the amount of engagement (i.e. reactions such as likes or shares) generated by the first communities in which memes appear and by every subsequent community. Since Facebook does not provide metrics such as view counts that would directly describe the amount of attention posts have received, we use engagement as a proxy for the visibility of posts. Figure 3 shows the first community where the meme accounts for a significant share of their total engagement. The memes also receive engagement from other communities but with diminishing returns. Differences in the relative sizes of communities do not explain the effect. While the mean number of accounts in the upstream communities (A1–A4) is 165.3, for downstream accounts (C1–C8) it is 494.7.

Even though memes receive the most engagement from the first cluster in which they appear, their overall reach still depends on them crossing clusters. Figure 4 describes how much of the meme's reach can be attributed to the first of the clusters. It shows that 32.1% of all engagement (across all clusters) results from posts in the first cluster. For the metric tracking the total number of posts that contained the meme, the share of the first cluster was smaller, 24.0%. These figures show that the potential reach of the memes is significantly higher if they can cross onto other clusters. The metric called duration measures the difference in time between the meme's first and last appearance in a particular cluster. It shows that memes survive and get reposted relatively long in their first cluster, but not as long as all clusters combined. The duration of memes in the first cluster was 59.1% of their duration overall.

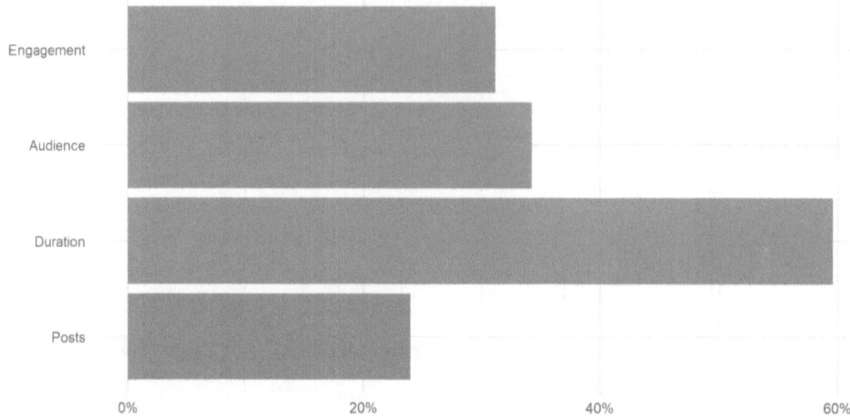

Fig. 4. The share of total engagement, audience, duration and number of posts for anti-vaccination memes that is attributed to the first community in which they appear

6   Discussion and Limitations

The results show that anti-vaccination memes typically first appeared on Facebook on accounts that opposed COVID-19 policies or focused on conspiracy theories about elites. From there, memes spread towards accounts associated with Conservative politics, especially the Republican party in the US and conservative parties in Canada and Australia. The results also show a regional pattern. Particularly US and Canadian accounts have international influence, as their memes spread into Europe, Africa and Australia. This paper contributes to the literature on online anti-vaccination discourse and the study of memes by being among the first to describe such large-scale regional patterns. We also describe a novel methodology for studying the spread of memes based on time-series data and the memes' text content.

There appears to be a change in the types of groups they reach when crossing regions. Particularly in Europe, we found they were associated with anti-systemic, extra-parliamentary political movements, while in Africa, the memes were shared in a wide range of "cultural" accounts. The difference between Europe, the US, and Canada may reflect that there typically was a broader consensus between parliamentary parties concerning lockdown and vaccination policies during the pandemic [1].

The results speak to the power of memes as a medium to cross between contexts and groups with very different agendas. In this respect, memes are like what Tuters calls "floating signifiers"; they are single images that can be used for various purposes and are "nevertheless temporarily united through affective bonds." [19]. This ability to move between different audiences is also what makes memes so influential. Our findings support this conclusion. They show that the first community in which memes appeared only accounted for about a third of the overall engagement they received.

The study has some limitations that future studies could overcome. We group memes based on their text content, mainly because this is a technical possibility offered by our data source, CrowdTangle. The use of CrowdTangle also meant some biases in the sample, especially the exclusion of smaller Facebook pages and groups. In some memes, the visual template stays the same while the text content changes. A different way of grouping memes may give different results. The study only covers 200 memes, which we identified by looking at trending posts based on English-language keywords. The keywords could have included other languages or the trademarks of vaccines that are specific to some regions. The identified patterns could have been different if we included a more extensive set of memes or other languages. We also describe different communities of accounts relatively coarsely through five categories. Another paper could explore in more detail the variety of accounts contained in every community and describe comparatively the differences between communities of accounts. In this study, we also did not have the opportunity to study the actual content of memes and how the contents may influence how they spread on social networks.

Notes on Funding. Kate Joynes-Burgess is funded by a Wellcome Trust PhD Studentship in the Humanities and Social Sciences.

References

1. Bol, D., Giani, M., Blais, A., Loewen, P.J.: The effect of COVID-19 lockdowns on political support: some good news for democracy? Eur. J. Polit. Res. **60**, 497–505 (2021). https://doi.org/10.1111/1475-6765.12401
2. CrowdTangle Team. CrowdTangle. Facebook, Menlo Park, California, United States. List ID: 1432547 (2021)
3. CrowdTangle: What data is CrowdTangle tracking? (2021). http://help.crowdtangle.com/en/articles/1140930-what-data-is-crowdtangle-tracking
4. De Zeeuw, D., Hagen, S., Peeters, S., Jokubauskaite, E.: Tracing normiefication. First Monday **25** (2020). https://doi.org/10.5210/fm.v25i11.10643
5. Gansner, E.R., Koutsofios, E., North, S.C., Vo, K.-P.: A technique for drawing directed graphs. IEEE Trans. Softw. Eng. **19**, 214–230 (1993). https://doi.org/10.1109/32.221135
6. Garett, R., Young, S.D.: Online misinformation and vaccine hesitancy. Transl. Behav. Med. **11**, 2194–2199 (2021). https://doi.org/10.1093/tbm/ibab128
7. Gutierrez-Bustamante, M., Espinosa-Leal, L.: Natural language processing methods for scoring sustainability reports—a study of Nordic listed companies. Sustainability **14**, 9165 (2022). https://doi.org/10.3390/su14159165
8. Holt, K.: Alternative media and the notion of anti-systemness: towards an analytical framework. Media Commun. 49–57 (2018). https://doi.org/10.17645/mac.v6i4.1467
9. Johnson, N.F., et al.: The online competition between pro- and anti-vaccination views. Nature **582**, 230–233 (2020). https://doi.org/10.1038/s41586-020-2281-1
10. Lemons, S., Linares López, C., Holte, R.C., Ruml, W.: Beam search: faster and monotonic. ICAPS **32**, 222–230 (2022). https://doi.org/10.1609/icaps.v32i1.19805
11. Marchal, N., Neudert, L.-M., Kollanyi, B., Howard, P.N.: Investigating visual content shared over Twitter during the 2019 EU parliamentary election campaign. Media Commun. **9**, 158–170 (2021). https://doi.org/10.17645/mac.v9i1.3421
12. Milani, E., Weitkamp, E., Webb, P.: The visual vaccine debate on Twitter: a social network analysis. Media Commun. **8**, 364–375 (2020). https://doi.org/10.17645/mac.v8i2.2847
13. Murtagh, F., Legendre, P.: Ward's hierarchical agglomerative clustering method: which algorithms implement Ward's criterion? J. Classif. **31**, 274–295 (2014). https://doi.org/10.1007/s00357-014-9161-z

14. Newman, M.: Networks: An Introduction. Oxford University Press, Oxford
15. Onnela, J.-P., et al.: Structure and tie strengths in mobile communication networks. Proc. Natl. Acad. Sci. **104**, 7332–7336 (2007). https://doi.org/10.1073/pnas.0610245104
16. Shifman, L.: Memes in Digital Culture. MIT Press (2013)
17. Sivakumar, V., Gordo, A., Paluri, M.: Rosetta: understanding text in images and videos with machine learning (2018). https://engineering.fb.com/2018/09/11/ai-research/rosetta-understanding-text-in-images-and-videos-with-machine-learning/
18. Thissen, D., Steinberg, L., Kuang, D.: Quick and easy implementation of the Benjamini-Hochberg procedure for controlling the false positive rate in multiple comparisons. J. Educ. Behav. Statist. **27**, 77–83 (2002). https://doi.org/10.3102/10769986027001077
19. Weng, L., Menczer, F., Ahn, Y.-Y.: Virality prediction and community structure in social networks. Sci. Rep. **3**, 2522 (2013). https://doi.org/10.1038/srep02522
20. Wiggins, B.E., Bowers, G.B.: Memes as genre: a structurational analysis of the memescape. New Media Soc. **17**, 1886–1906 (2015). https://doi.org/10.1177/1461444814535194
21. Woolf, B.: The log likelihood ratio test (the G-test). Ann. Hum. Genet. **21**, 397–409 (1957). https://doi.org/10.1111/j.1469-1809.1972.tb00293.x

Multi-platform Framing Analysis: A Case Study of Kristiansand Quran Burning

Anna-Katharina Jung[1] , Gautam Kishore Shahi[1(✉)] , Jennifer Fromm[1],
Kari Anne Røysland[2], and Kim Henrik Gronert[3]

[1] University of Duisburg-Essen, Duisburg, Germany
gautam.shahi@uni-due.de
[2] University of Agder, Kristiansand, Norway
[3] Kristiansand Kommune, Kristiansand, Norway

Abstract. The framing of events in various media and discourse spaces is crucial in the era of misinformation and polarization. Many studies, however, are limited to specific media or networks, disregarding the importance of cross-platform diffusion. This study overcomes that limitation by conducting a multi-platform framing analysis on Twitter, YouTube, and traditional media analyzing the 2019 Koran burning in Kristiansand, Norway. It examines media and policy frames and uncovers network connections through shared URLs. The findings show that online news emphasizes the incident's legality, while social media focuses on its morality, with harsh hate speech prevalent in YouTube comments. Additionally, YouTube is identified as the most self-contained community, whereas Twitter is the most open to external inputs.

Keywords: Quran burning · Framing Theory · Frame Analysis · Cross-platform diffusion · Harmful content

1 Introduction

The appearance and rise of social media platforms restructured and diversified the process of information diffusion. While priorly, the dissemination of information was limited to traditional media outlets managed by gatekeeping journalists, nowadays, information can be produced and shared by everyone with online access [1]. As a result of this development, journalists have not only lost their major influence on the dissemination of content but also the sovereignty of interpretation. The classification of content is in the hands of every single online actor. The process of highlighting certain elements of a piece of content and promoting a particular understanding and interpretation is known as the concept of framing [2]. Although the media landscape is diverse, previous research on framing and information diffusion often focused only on one specific social media platform or traditional news outlets [3]. With our study, we aim to advance multi-platform framing of societal incidents. The case of the Quran burning in Kristiansand, Norway is used as an example in our study to demonstrate the application and

M. Preuss et al. (Eds.): MISDOOM 2024, LNCS 15175, pp. 101–130, 2024.
https://doi.org/10.1007/978-3-031-71210-4_7

diffusion of media frames throughout different types of online media platforms. On 16th November 2019, Lars Thorsen - the leader of the Norwegian Anti-Islam group Stop the Islamification of Norway (SIAN), attempted to burn the Quran on the main square of Kristiansand. Several persons attacked Lars Thorsen to stop him from burning the Quran and were arrested by the police. About 300 people witnessed the incident, and shortly afterwards, videos of the Quran burning and the attacks circulated on the net. The incident was heavily discussed in both online news sources and social media. While many members of the Muslim community described the attackers as defenders of Islam, other actors rather expressed anti-Islamist views. These different media frames resulted in tensions within Norwegian society and considerable problems for the Norwegian government. We aim to answer the following research questions:

RQ1: How was the Quran burning incident in Kristiansand framed on different social media platforms (Twitter (now X), YouTube) and on online news sites? RQ2: How is the diffusion between the different social media platforms and online news sites shaped?

For this multi-platform framing analysis, we analyzed 1,136 tweets, 71 YouTube videos with 2,031 comments, and 109 articles from online news sources. We distinguish between social media that allows any user to create and share content and online news sites where editorial teams retain control over the publication of articles and associated comments [4]. It should be noted that online news sites differ in the extent to which they follow the ethical code of practice for the press adopted by the Norwegian Press Association. The study is organized as follows. First, a short insight into the development and methodical approaches to the framing theory are presented, followed by a concise overview of multi-platform framing and cross-platform diffusion. Afterwards, the methodical approach is presented. Summarizing the case study, the approach to data collection and cleaning, such as the description of the coding procedure and code book. This is followed by the presentation of the results, giving an overview about the distribution of frames on the different platforms, such as Uniform Resource Locator (URL) analysis. In the discussion section, connections to the state of the art presented and prior research are drawn. This discussion section is followed by a short overview about the limitations of the study and the ideas for future research. The study is rounded off by the presentation of the conclusion in which the main findings and the answers to the research questions are summarized.

2   State of the Art

In this section, we describe framing theory, multi-platform framing and Cross platform information diffusion.

2.1   Framing Theory

The theory of framing was originally created in the field of sociology in the 1950s and has been refined ever since by various disciplines ranging from psychology to political and media studies [5–7]. As well in the more technical field of information systems, the framing theory has been adapted to approach the analysis of stakeholder perspectives in a technological context, or to analyze communication in online environments [3, 8] One of the most comprehensive definitions of framing was provided by the political scientist Robert Entman: "Framing essentially involves selection and salience. To frame is to select some aspects of a perceived reality and make them more salient in a communication text, in such a way as to promote a particular problem definition, causal interpretation, moral evaluation and/or treatment recommendation for the item described" ([2], p. 52). Thus, framing looks not only at the issues and topics covered by the media but also at the angles being taken. As diverse as the disciplines that adapted the framing theory are the methodological approaches that have been developed for its analysis. The operationalization of frames for empirical studies is complex and challenging, among other things, due to the huge amount of data that needs to be annotated (manually) and the influence of personal interpretation of media and its frames [9]. In prior research, authors divide the existing methodological approaches to frame analysis in deductive approaches (based on priorly formulated frames) and inductive approaches (based on frames derived from the specific data set in focus) [9]. While studies solely based on deductive frame categories are very systematic and can be easily replicated, they have the shortcoming that they might ignore important information within the data set if it does not fit the priorly defined frames [10]. In contrast to that, inductive approaches use the data and its context as a basis for the creation of frames and thus are much more sensitive to the peculiarities of specific research cases [11]. In our study, we applied a mixture of deductive and inductive approaches to the framing analysis. As a basis, we used the codebook for analysis of media frames within and across policy issues by [12, 13] and modified it according to the cultural and thematic context. The codebook will be explained in more detail in the method section.

2.2   Multi-platform Framing

While journalists and traditional media houses still have a huge impact on the shaping of public debates, the influence of online users not bound to news values and reporting standards has increased with the rise of social networks and hybrid media systems [14]. This development is described as networked gatekeeping and networked framing and was defined by [15] as the involvement of a diversity of online actors from many different backgrounds, including journalists, activists, non-elite media supporters and regular users, who gained prominence and attention in their network by effective communicative and social practices to spread their messages. Networked framing, like networked gatekeeping, stands for the prominence interpretations received via crowdsourcing actions [15]. Although [15] value the difference between gatekeeping and framing in social networks within their own research on the revolution in Egypt, they fully focus on the discourse on Twitter and thus miss out on giving an overview of the process on multiple platforms. As well studies incorporating the idea of networked publics and framing mainly limited their scope to one platform, as for example [16] who mapped the discussion on the Iranian presidential elections 2017 on Twitter [16], depicting the different groups of online elites discussing the subject or previous research [17] which analyzed the discourse on migration during the Canadian elections 2019. Another recent example is the analysis of [18] who analyzed the hijacking and reframing of the MeToo hashtag by right-wing actors in a multi-national Twitter analysis. While [18] do involve different languages and thus different national communities on Twitter, they did disregard other media outlets than Twitter. One of the very few studies which pays attention to the research gap of multi-platform framing is [19], which analyzed the discourse about the refugee crisis in the Finish online news media and social media [19]. In contrast to the present study, a computational topic and framing detection were applied, and a latent Dirichlet allocation algorithm was used. While the scope of our study is similar, the methodical approaches differ from each other.

2.3   Cross Platform Information Diffusion

The sharing and presentation of frames within one network and across platform boarders can be as well described as a form of information diffusion. Information diffusion can be defined "as the process by which a piece of information (knowledge) is spread and reaches individuals through interactions" [20]. On social media, this process depends on individuals who spread information through retweets, shares and likes. The information created by verified accounts spreads faster than non-verified sources [21,22]. One stream of information diffusion research takes a micro perspective and aims to understand why individual users distribute information [23,24]. For example, authors in prior research [24] found that learning and social engagement are the most important motivations for content sharing [24]. Another stream of research examines the phenomenon from a macro perspective, focusing on predicting how information spreads through a social network. These studies often aim to assess and improve information diffusion models such as information cascade or threshold models [25–28]. To understand information diffusion, scholars highlighted the importance of analyzing the interplay of different actor and content characteristics [29]. Actor-centered studies demonstrated the power of opinion leaders in the information diffusion process [30,31] and distinguish between different roles such as information starters, information amplifiers, and information transmitters [32]. Other studies rather highlighted the impact of content characteristics such as emotionality [33] or the attachment of images and videos [3]. Notably, most previous studies focused on a single platform such as Twitter, thereby neglecting the reality of information diffusion, as is also the case for networked framing. In this regard, [34] already argued that social media users can share content from Facebook to Twitter and vice versa, pointing toward the vanishing boundaries between different social media platforms. A study proposed that sharing viral videos on alternative platforms might affect their popularity on the original platform [35]. Furthermore, scholars found a significant influence of mass media and external websites on information diffusion within a social media platform

[36]. This phenomenon is also known as the spill-over effect among communication scientists [37]. The detection of spill-over effects represents a methodological challenge as it is difficult to find the origin of information in the online media sphere [38]. The authors suggested using a crawler to identify URLs linking to other online information sources. Jung et al. [3] built upon this methodological approach and demonstrated in a case study that online news sites referenced more frequently to information from Twitter than vice versa. With our study, we aim to extend the scarce research body on multi-platform networked framing and cross-platform diffusion by examining the occurrence and diffusion of frames within and across social media and online media.

3 Research Design

In this section, we explain the steps involved in performing the study. They are discussed below.

3.1 Data Collection

In this section, we explain the data collection from different platforms. For a holistic picture of the online discourse, Twitter and YouTube, as well as Norwegian newspapers, were chosen. While Twitter is known for textual breaking news content, YouTube is the most prominent platform for video content. Therefore, these two social networks were considered especially useful for this study. The time frame for the data collection was 12th November 2019 until 30th November 2019. A detailed explanation of each platform is given below. For all platforms, we decided that the keyword *SIAN*, as the organizer of the event, such as the keywords *Arne Tumyr* and *Lars Thorsen*, as the involved SIAN leaders, were relevant. Furthermore, the keyword koranbrenning was chosen as it was the most prevalent term to describe the event in the Norwegian news. Finally *Kristiansand* was chosen as a keyword, as the incident's location. The results of the data collection confirmed that the keywords delivered relevant results, wherefore the keyword selection was not further adjusted.

Twitter Data. The Twitter data was gathered with a self-developed Python crawler, which connects to the Twitter Search Application Programming Interface (API) before the commercialization of Twitter data) and collects tweets using keywords SIAN, Arne Tumyr, Lars Thorsen, koranbrenning. The tool collected all Norwegian tweets, retweets, and replies that contained at least one of these keywords and were published from 12th November 2019 until 30th November 2019. We manually checked the search results for relevance and excluded 57 tweets that were not related to the Quran burning in Kristiansand, excluding tweets about another Quran burning that happened in Sweden or tweets about other activities of SIAN, Arne Tumyr, and Lars Thorsen. The final dataset included 2,267 tweets consisting of 865 original tweets, 1,131 retweets, 224 replies, and 47 commented retweets. The 1,131 retweets were excluded from analysis and treated as duplicates as they did not add new frames to the Twitter discourse. The final Twitter data set contained 1,136 tweets.

News Paper Articles. For tracking the news media, we used commercial software by M-brain (now Valona[1]) to monitor media, ensuring comprehensive news coverage. It provided us with openly accessible content and those behind online paywalls. We used the search terms "koranbrenning" and "Kristiansand" to browse the content from the news media. M-brain searched all Norwegian media outlets and returned the articles which match the search terms. From the obtained results, we further filtered the news articles which contained any of the search terms "Lars Thorsen", "Arne Tumyr", or "SIAN". The final news media data set included 115 news articles that had been published between 12th November 2019 and 30th November 2019. After duplicates were deleted, 109 articles remained for the analysis. The data set included the article heading, URL to the news article, and date of publication, and we crawled the content of the news article. The media outlets can be categorized into three groups: State-owned and mainstream media, Online and Independent Media and Special Interest and Non-News Platforms. In addition, we also added to this classification who owned the media outlet and their affiliation to the Norwegian Press Organization, such additional notes if applicable. For a detailed overview please refer to Table @reftab2 in the Appendix.

YouTube Videos and Comments. For the YouTube analysis, we collected videos and comments related to the Quran Burning incident. To identify the relevant videos, we used the YouTube keyword search and conducted four different manual searches of the keywords "SIAN Norway," "Arne Tumyr," "Lars Thorsen," and "Koranbrenning." The relevancy was assessed by reading the title and description and watching the video. Some videos were excluded, for example, when the videos were related to a different Quran burning incident. Videos that occurred in multiple searches because they included several keywords were included only once. Overall, we excluded five duplicate videos. We identified 112 relevant videos in total. Out of them, 71 videos had comments. We crawled all 8,917 comments related to those videos. As the total number of comments was too extensive for a manual assessment, we applied a sampling approach to all videos with more than 100 comments. Ten videos had more than 100 comments, and 62 videos had less than 100 comments. For the sampling, we took all comments from the videos with less than 100 comments, and for videos that had more than 100 comments, we sampled 100 comments from each video. Overall, we got 2,031 comments from 71 videos in total. This approach provided us with a diverse data set of all comments from all videos. In contrast to the newspaper articles and tweets regarding the Collection of YouTube videos and comments, there was no language restriction to Norwegian and English, but all videos and comments have been analysed with help of the subtitles provided by YouTube and translation software whenever possible.

---

[1] https://valonaintelligence.com/.

3.2   Data Analysis and Preprocessing

In this section, we describe the steps involved in the data preprocessing and analysis. We have applied a series of steps to clean our data set. We filtered the URLs from the text of tweets, YouTube comments, and news articles for data cleaning following the approach mentioned in [39]. After that, we manually identified the domain of the URLs to identify the link target platforms (i.e., Twitter, YouTube, online news sources, and others). The category others included links leading to other social media and online news sources that we have not included in our sample (e.g., Facebook, Instagram, religious websites).

3.3   Frame Analysis

As the Quran Burning incident in Kristiansand can be classified as a politically motivated event, we decided to use an existing codebook for the analysis of policy frames by [12,13]. The codebook has been developed and validated with a pilot study covering three major events in the US. We used the most recent version of the codebook, which was updated in 2016. The codebook was developed for the analysis of policy debates in the United States and consists of 15 frame dimensions. The 15 frame dimensions have been adapted according to the Norwegian context and the context of the Quran Burning incident. Each dimension was equipped with a short paragraph about the relevance of the Quran Burning case, possible keywords, and examples, which can be found in Table @reftab1 in Appendix. As the data from Twitter, YouTube and newspaper articles confronted us with different conditions the codebook was slightly adapted for each medium, which will be explained along the description of the coding process. As a first step of the framing analysis, the coders intensively studied the codebook and then added relevant paragraphs, keywords, and examples. In the next step the coders have been provided with the data sets and their English translations. After reading the text, the coders needed to decide if the translation was understandable or if there was further clarification needed. In case there was a better translation of Norwegian data required, the Norwegian team members were involved. If the translation was understandable, coders needed to decide if the information was relevant for the respective case study. To understand the YouTube videos, the subtitle function was used if available, and the title and description were translated with the help of Google Translate. Afterwards, the relevance of the data was evaluated. The first relevant criterion was whether the tweet, video or comment was about or in connection with the Quran burning in Kristiansand. If this was not the case, it was not deemed to be relevant. Exceptions were made if the covered international incident was a reaction to the Quran Burning in Kristiansand. Messages which only contained an emoticon or random strings of characters were marked as irrelevant. The tweets of the Twitter data set have been sorted according to the respective tweet ID in order to identify the conversational threads to which they belonged. Each tweet, YouTube video, YouTube comment, or newspaper article received one primary frame. The frame could vary from the original tweet in case of commented retweets and replies. In case of more complex messages, especially regarding newspaper articles a secondary frame was chosen if it was not possible to reduce the main messages of the text to one primary frame. Each data set was coded by two coders. First of all, 20% of each data set was coded independently to check the intercoder reliability of each coding. The intercoder reliability was calculated in the form of Cohen's Kappa coefficient which can be found in Table @reftab4 of Appendix. If the result was satisfying, the coding process was continued. In case of deviations in the first coding round, a third coder was involved, and the majority rule has been applied. The rest of the data sets were divided between the first two coders.

4   Result

In section, we explain the result obtained from the different analyses to answer the research questions.

4.1   Framing Analysis

With help of the code book we identified the different frames, which have been used in the discourse and media coverage about the Quran burning incident in Kristiansand. We have seen a distinct usage of frames in news articles, tweets and YouTube videos and comments. A detailed description of annotated frames is given in Table @reftab3 in the Appendix. For the news articles, primary frames and secondary frames have been applied regularly, as the longer texts often did not allow being reduced to one single frame. For the coding of the YouTube comments the frame dimension "None" was applied more frequently than in comparison to the other media types. By having a closer look at this frame we realized that this was the case because many of the comments could not be translated for analysis and the automated translation had reached its limits. In the 109 coded news articles, the frame dimension Legality, Constitutionality & Jurisdiction was most frequently used, with 50 (45.9%) references. That means that most of the news articles had legal issues as their main subject in the form of references to freedom of speech or constitutional issues. Very prevalent was the discussion if it was legal, according to the Norwegian constitution, to burn the Quran. One example of the use of the legality frame dimension is an article by the online news outlet document.no, with the title "It should not be allowed to burn holy books". The article discussed if the decision by the Police Directorate to stop SIAN from burning a copy of the Quran, as a violation of section 185 of the Penal Code on the prohibition of hate speech, was well grounded. The second most applied frame dimension in the news article data set was the External Regulation and Reputation frame with 12%. The incident in Kristiansand led to direct reactions in the Muslim world, especially Pakistan. The articles in which this frame was used often discussed the implications of the Quran burning for the Norwegian telephone provider Telenor, which owns more than a quarter of the Pakistani cellular market [38]. The public service broadcaster NRK published an article with the title "Call for boycott of Norwegian companies after Quran burning". The article described the reactions in the Pakistani community and media landscape to boycott Norwegian products and especially the Pakistani branch of the Norwegian telephone provider Telenor. In addition to that, articles with the External Regulation and Reputation frame described the political reactions to the incident in the form of an appointment of the Norwegian ambassador in Pakistan for a statement on the case by Prime Minister Imran Khan and the Ministry of Foreign Affairs. An example for that is the article "Norway is called on the carpet" (the Norwegian proverb to call someone to the carpet, can be translated with "to scold someone") by the Norwegian daily newspaper Dagbladet. It discussed that the Pakistani Ministry of Foreign Affairs scolded Norway's ambassador and expressed concern that a Quran was set on fire in Kristiansand. The frame dimension Security and Defense was with 10.1% also applied regularly in the news article data set. The articles, which contained this primary frame, discussed extensively that the Quran burning incident resulted in a concrete security threat for the Norwegian state. One outlet which used this frame is e.. the news site resett.no, which is a controversial online news site in Norway, known for its skepticism regarding immigration and Islam. Resett.no is not part of the Norwegian Press Organization due to the fact that the organization has deemed that they do not adhere to the Norwegian Press Codex. The article of resett.no using the Security and Defense frame has the title: "Threatened to kill after Quran burning: Kill him please!" It discussed that the burning of the Quran has created violent reactions both on social media, but also from Muslim communities in Norway. The article stated that several Muslim leaders in Agder warned that they will now report SIAN to the police. Besides that, the Security and Defense frame was applied in articles, which reported about protest actions, which were triggered by the incident. One example for that is the article "The Norwegian flag is burned in protest against the burning of the Quran" by the local newspaper Fedrelandsvennen, which reported that the Norwegian flag was burned during demonstrations in different Muslim countries among others in the state of Karachi in Pakistan. The authors interpreted these incidents as a sign of a concrete threat against the Norwegian state to suffer an Islamist-motivated attack. Due to the complexity of the newspaper articles in several cases a secondary frame was chosen. The most common secondary frame was again Legality, Constitutionality & Jurisdiction with (32%), which underlines the importance of the legality frame in the news article data set. Besides that as well the Morality and Ethics (18%), Political Factors and Implications (16%) and Security and Defense (14%) frames played an important role as secondary frames. The article "Koran burning, blasphemy, freedom of speech and hate speech" is an example of an article with a primary and a secondary frame. The primary frame is Legality, Constitutionality & Jurisdiction and the secondary frame is Morality and Ethics. The article discusses both the legal interpretation of the incident and its morality, following the stance that not everything which is legal is as well morally defensible.

4.2   Tweets

Of the 1,136 analyzed tweets, 47 tweets were coded as irrelevant, which are 4% of the data set. Among the relevant tweets, the Morality and Ethics frame was with 28.1% the top frame. An anchor example for this category is: "I am not a true follower, but what if the Bible was burned? Would antifa violence responders react? I doubt.". In addition to the Morality and Ethics frame the Political Factors and Implications frame dimension was used in 19.2% of the sample. There have been a lot of comments after the event which underlined a political motivation. Both lay people and politicians used the burning of the Quran to voice political views, coming from different political camps. Several accounts pointed out that they have the impression that SIAN received more attention, that it deserved according to their overall importance for the Norwegian political landscape. One anchor example for that is: "Given that the only Norwegian party of significance that is close to SIAN has just made a historically poor municipal election, SIAN should not imagine that they have any significant support." The accounts, who advocated for SIAN often pointed out that SIAN is a relevant political group. In the following example SIAN is presented as a moderate, non violent group in comparison to political groups of the left political spectrum: "Then you should stop using the word extremist about SIAN. They have never resorted to violence, which your dear Communists in Red and Antifa constantly do". Besides that, only the Legality frame reached a relevant number of tweets with 13.6%. Two examples for the usage of the Legality, Constitutionality & Jurisdiction frame are:

"Penal Code §185 used against burning of the Quran? Seems like the law stretches quite a bit." and "Norwegian scandal: Freedom of speech is something we play. The police had received a secret illegal order to stop "violation of the Qur'an" when the SIAN demonstration in Kristiansand was brutally interrupted by local police." For annoated tweets without none frame, around 16% (191 tweets) of all tweets referred to external media sources. 55 of those tweets have been published by media organizations themselves, the others were shared by mainly individual accounts and some organizations. As these tweets neutrally shared media links, with short article snippets instead the content of the shared media content was coded for the analysis. All other frames covered only in between 0.2% and 7.3% of the data set and are thus not described in more detail. A second frame added to less than 5% of the tweets and can thus be ignored.

4.3   YouTube Videos

All YouTube videos that only showed the incident as a whole without commenting on it were coded as None if there was no frame included either in the title or description of the video. The Morality and Ethics frame was the most prevalent frame used in the YouTube videos, with 36.6%. However, a minor number of videos applied to the External Regulations & Reputation frame, which together account for 9.9% of the data set.

Fig. 1. Annotated YouTube videos(From left to right video a, b, c)

The video in Fig. 1 (a) was uploaded to YouTube by channel JHUNJHUNU PRIME TIME, joined YouTube on the 7th of November 2019, only a few days prior to the incident. Even if the account is supposed to give the impression of an official station due to the name and the chosen avatar, it can be assumed that it is not an official source but a channel run by a private person. Another indicator for that is that the channel description is incomplete. Another example for the use of the morality frame is (b) in Fig. 1 a video of the leader of the Norwegian PEGIDA (Patriotic Europeans against the Islamization of the Occident). In his video with the title "SIAN's Koran burning in Kristiansand; what does the quran say¿', which he prepared in reaction to the SIAN burning of the Quran in Kristiansand, he presents his interpretation of the five pillars of the Quran. This video is a good anchor example for videos which have been created by sympathizers of SIAN. The videos, which belonged to the External Regulation and Reputation frame, often showed and described protests, which came up in Muslim countries, especially Pakistan, after the incident. An anchor example can be the following video. This video (c) in Fig. 1 was posted by the account Pinpoint Pakistan, which has a relatively professional appearance, such as JHUNJHUNU PRIME TIME. The channel contains more information about its scope and gives a contact email for questions. However, there is only a YouTube and Facebook Page with the name of this organization and no official media house under this name, which as well gives the impression that it is a media channel run by private persons. It needs to be doubted that the video thus has been produced by the channel owners themselves.

4.4 YouTube Comments

Coding the YouTube comments, we used fewer frames than the other channels, pointing as well at the limitations of using a predefined codebook. The frames that were most used were Morality and Ethics, None and Other. The reason why Morality and Ethics was the most frequently used, was the reference to religion, e.g.: "Long live Allah." Often the morality frame was also used to express beliefs in a hateful manner: "I pissed in koran and ur momz!". In the frame Other we have put comments that did not fit in any other category, but were still relevant. Often there was shortly formulated support or dislike formulated in a very short manner like "Good" or "Nice" or "lionhearted" or from the SIAN supporters: "Thanks Lars". Some have also been hate speech like: "Look at the red pig he looks like". The reason why so many comments were coded as none, was because the content either did not make sense, or we did not understand the meaning of it. While some meaning might have been lost in translation, there have been comments including random combinations of letters. We also saw 5.2% of comments about Norway's reputation, so we coded these External Regulation and Reputation. Examples are "Fuck Norway, boycott Norway", "Norwegians are bastards" and "Shame on Norway". This could have harmed Norway's reputation and were often as well in a hate speech manner.

4.5   URL Analysis

We coded 888 tweets, 27 YouTube comments, and 68 news articles during the manual framing analysis, including reference hyperlinks from one of the other platforms. However, some tweets, comments, and articles included multiple URLs. Summing up, those that included more than one URL led to the total number of 988 URLs from tweets, 27 from YouTube comments, and 456 URLs from news articles from the above spillover links. If there were multiple URLs from one tweet, YouTube comment, or newspaper article to another platform, we split it into different URLs, so only a link is associated with each source and the target node. We further analyzed the domain of the URLs to get information about the spillover of hyperlinks. To identify cross-platform diffusion and spillover effects, we categorize the URLs into four categories based on domains: Twitter, YouTube, News Media, and others (which include other domains apart from the above three, like social media platforms Facebook and Instagram.). Figure 2 describes the number of different URLs shared from one platform to another. The figure shows the diffusion of URLs from each platform to four different categories: Twitter to news media, YouTube, Twitter and others. Overall, news articles contain multiple URLs within the articles, mainly referring to other news articles. On Twitter the tweet authors as well use references within the own network boundaries by referencing tweets, but as well share URLs of news media and YouTube. In contrast YouTube contains limited URLs, mainly staying within own network boundaries.

Within our collected datasets, we analysed the spillover of URLs among news articles, Twitter and YouTube. We matched URLs of news articles to Twitter and YouTube. A spillover of URLs from news article to another is observed mainly on Twitter; around 26% unique news articles are posted 171 times on Twitter from domains such as *utrop.no, resett.no, gjenstridig.no, nrk.no, dagladet.no, document.no, afternposten, vg.no, rights.no, nrk.no.* At the same time, only two news articles are shared on YouTube comments, which are not explicitly from our datasets. For cross-platform, 17 YouTube videos are shared on Twitter. In contrast, among YouTube comments, only a few URLs are mentioned in comments, mainly on other YouTube videos and some other social media platforms such as Facebook and VK.

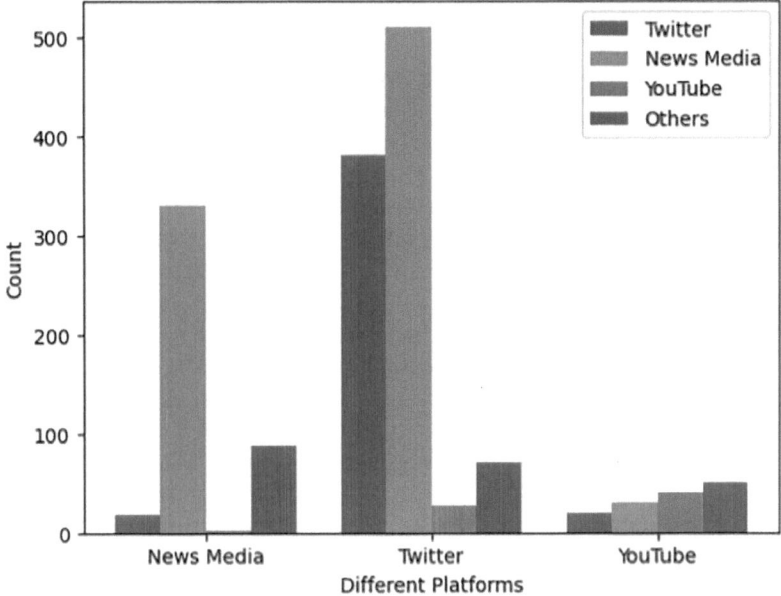

Fig. 2. Distribution of URLs and their source on three different platforms.

5   Discussion

This study offers insights about two main topics: differences of multi platform framing of a social incident on social media (Twitter and YouTube) and online news sites (RQ1) and cross-platform diffusion of topics and frames (RQ2). The content analysis of the online news site articles, tweets, and YouTube videos and comments resulted in a distinctive application of frame dimensions on the different platforms. Of the 14 main frame dimensions adapted from Boydstun et al. [12], only four frame dimensions reached a threshold of at least 10% in one of the data sets, namely Legality, Morality, External relations, Political factors and the two dimensions None and Other. While the legality frame dominated the discourse on online news sites, the morality frame dominated the two social media data sets. We argue that the high dominance of the morality frame in the social media data sets is related to the higher level of personal communication on social media platforms, which allows each individual and organization to contribute to the discussion [1]. According to [40] moral intuition forms the very basis of any normative evaluation [40]. It is an unfiltered and non-reflected reaction if an incident should be classified as right or wrong [41]. We argue that the use of the morality and ethics frame might be more prevalent in social media as individual users are more likely to express their moral intuition than (professional) journalists. Further, we considered international sources in the YouTube data set too, wherefore here we also see reactions from people living in Muslim countries like Pakistan, feeling morally offended. The harshest formulation of personal opinions was present in the analyzed YouTube comments, which involved only the frame dimensions of morality and other. The other category was used particularly frequently for YouTube comments, including hate speech which could not be assigned to any of the existing frame dimensions. Furthermore, YouTube comments showed the highest level of polarization, particularly within the morality frame. This polarization is reflected by potential echo chambers of the Muslim supporters and right-wing supporters, predominantly encountering viewpoints that reinforce their existing beliefs, which might intensify polarization. The dominance of the morality frame, which provokes strong emotional responses, contributes to this phenomenon. Polarization can have broader societal impacts, including increased social tensions and greater distance between different groups or countries. The problem of misinformation, which is linked to highly polarized discourse environments, extends beyond false information to the intensive diffusion of specific frames and narratives that shape public beliefs and perceptions [42]. According to Starbird, these frames influence the evidence used in sensemaking processes and guide interpretations and the formation of public opinion. Our results suggest that the frames and narratives surrounding the Quran burning event may overshadow existing evidence, exacerbating societal and political polarization. However, the analysis of the Twitter comments revealed as well the limitations regarding the application of Boydstun's codebook on YouTube comments. In further research, a more specific codebook should be developed for this medium and discourse space. The fact that polarization was less prevalent on Twitter could potentially be explained by the different user groups of the platforms, or differently strict or successful countermeasures of the platforms regarding hate speech [43]. The deletion of hate speech should be practiced more strongly by YouTube. Not only at the video level but, above all, in the comments, where AI-supported approaches may be used. The perspective in the YouTube comments was very unified and contained mainly narratives like the attackers of SIAN are heroes, Islam is a religion that should be praised, and Norway should be reproached for not respecting and protecting Islam. We argue that due to the language barriers, as most of these comments have been originally published in Urdu or Arabic, there was little variation and counterspeech of different opinion camps. Research has shown that users do interact barely with textual posts in foreign languages [44]. While passive interactions in the form of likes happen, commenting takes place very rarely [43]. Therefore, we assume that Norwegian or English-speaking YouTube users have not engaged and reacted with the comments in Arabic or Urdu, which explains the non-existent counter speech. It also explains a different application and diffusion of frames within different user/language groups and shows that the idea of networked publics and the networked framing has certain boundaries [15]. However, the traditional media act as a bridge actor here, presenting the incidents of hatred from social media in other countries such as official reactions from countries such as Pakistan (External relations frame), which underlines the role of traditional news media in cross platform frame diffusion. In contrast to YouTube and the online news sources the discourse on Twitter was the most diverse according to the variety of applied frames, although the threshold of 10% was not exceeded for all frame dimensions. It indicates that Twitter might represent a more diverse discourse space compared to the other platforms. However, this should always be considered with the caveat that the topic itself may also have influenced how it was discussed on which platform. For further generalizations future studies are indispensable. Based on the Kristiansand incident, we perceived it as unexpected that meta-discourses under the frames of Fairness and Equality or Cultural Identity did not play a serious role in the data set. There was also no difference in the online news sources, which offer more space for societal discourses. Instead of an overall societal discussion about the role of Islam and Muslim groups in Norwegian society, the discussion was more focused on the personal moral classification of the conflict, or in online news sources on the legality of the committed act. This points to a potential question for future research to which extent social networks allow and foster meta-discourses or whether these are lost in the mass of personal statements. After analyzing the distribution of the different frames among the three analyzed platforms (Twitter, YouTube and online news sites), the analysis of URLs used in the data set was implemented to answer RQ2. First, we categorized the links originating from a platform according to their platform type: Twitter, YouTube, news articles, and others. The category others included all links that did not fit the three main categories and included i.e. references to Instagram, Facebook, and religious websites (e.g. islam.net). We observed that a significant amount of URLs diffusion is happening within the same platform for news articles and YouTube comments. While around 67% of all URLs in YouTube comments point to other YouTube content, 72% of all online news sources point to other online news sources while only 39% of URLs mentioned in tweets refer to other tweets. Around 47% of URLs mentioned in collected news articles refer to the same media house, which indicates that online news sources are more likely to share sources from their own company to strengthen their own economic goals of longer dwell time and clicks. Solely on Twitter, 52% URLs mentioned in tweets refers to news media, 3% to YouTube, 39% to other tweets and 8% to other platforms. This strengthens the ideas of [31,36], who identified news media as influential drivers of diffusion in social networks. In contrast, the URLs of news sites in the Quran Burning case study only included roughly 8% of the URLs pointing to different social media sites, including Twitter and Facebook. This contradicts the findings of Jung (2018) [3], who found out that news media were referencing Twitter more often than Twitter posts referred to news media. However, Jung (2018) [3] did not use a data set looking at one specific case study but a broader variation of topics. Although the diffusion and referencing within the respective platform boundaries are high, cross-platform diffusion makes up 25–60% of the sub datasets of this case study, strengthening the results of [34,35], who both found an interdependence between the degree of diffusion and cross-platform spill-overs. While for the spill over of news articles to Twitter it could be identified by our coding, that in many cases shared news articles also led to a share of frames, as snippets of the articles formed as well part of the tweet, it remains unclear is if the other reference spill-overs which have been identified in the data sets do also directly lead to a frame spill-over, which could give insights into the importance of the different platforms and actors involved in the frame-setting and agenda-building process [38].

6   Limitations and Future Research

One major limitation of our keyword-based data collection approach is that some relevant data about the Quran burning incident in Kristiansand might have been missed, compromising completeness. Furthermore, the fact that an existing code-book was adapted, may be another methodical limitation. A codebook derived from the data set always has the strength of being more case-related and specific. While the Twitter data and YouTube videos could be easily coded with the media corpus codebook, We see the limitations of the codebook for YouTube comments and understand an adoption of it for YouTube comments as a potential future research endeavor. We admit that there is a certain language bias in relation to the collection of YouTube videos and comments in our analysis. However, we argue that videos are more accessible across languages compared to text alone, and AI-generated subtitles on YouTube were sufficiently accurate for our analysis. In addition to the limitations the study also stimulates many new ideas for further research. First, in a follow-up study, it would make sense to code not only the dataset collected in the first step, but also all the third-party content identified by the URL analysis on the three platforms. Through this snowball system, it would be possible to make clearer statements about frame spill-overs in the future. This further analysis could for example be supported by a network analysis to visualize the spill-overs in the different directions and could help to identify the main frame-setters. Furthermore, it would be interesting to investigate whether sockpuppeting or astroturfing took place to push certain frames (e.g. by following the approach presented in [44]. Furthermore, it would also be appropriate to focus on the questions raised in the discussion of this article on the topic of discourse diversity on different platforms and the possibility of meta-discourses in social networks.

7   Conclusion

This study contributes to closing the research gap of networked framing on multiple platforms by analyzing how the socially and politically relevant incident of the Quran burning by the Anti-Islamic group SIAN in Kristiansand was framed on Twitter, YouTube and in online news sources. The analysis revealed that on social media the frame dimension of morality and ethics was highly dominant, while on online news sites the legality frame played the most relevant role. The higher use of the morality frame on social networks can be related to two main reasons: the higher number of personal statements in social networks and the involvement of users from Islamic states like Pakistan who were morally concerned by the incident. Another finding was the high appearance of hate speech in the form of the other frame dimension in the YouTube comments, which was not similarly present on other platforms. As most hate speech was published in Urdu and Arabic there was no counter-speech in English or Norwegian, underlining a lack of interaction between different language groups and ergo a limited diffusion of frames between different language groups. Which underlines the limits of the proposed concept of networked framing and gatekeeping by [15]. Although the internationality of the social media users was higher on YouTube, the frame dimension of External regulations and & Reputation was more relevant in online news sources. However, online news sources were highly dominated by the legality frame, discussing the legal classification of the incident in accordance with the Norwegian law, which did only play a minor role on social networking sites. The highest diversity of frame dimensions was applied by the Twitter community pointing at a more manifold discussion of the topic on this platform. However, meta-discourses on the fairness of the treatment of minority groups or a discussion on the cultural identity of Norwegian society in relation to the incident have been absent. Concerning the diffusion of content regarding the Quran Burning incident between different social media platforms and online news sites, it could be revealed that most diffusion takes place within the specific network boundaries. On Twitter, the highest amount of content generated outside the platform boundaries was shared. The most self-contained platform in this study was YouTube, which leads to the assumption that, at least for this case study, YouTube has a limited networked public solely looking at the content created by its own community. Cross-platform diffusion forms between a quarter to two thirds of the disseminated content, which underlines the interconnectedness and influence between the different discourse spaces and platforms. The study underscores the discursive power of social network users, who do not solely copy the frames of traditional media one-to-one but apply different and more multifaceted frames in their reflections. The greatest linkage was found between Twitter and online news sources for which we could identify not only a reference- but as well frame spill-over, as to a great extent frames of the news sources were spilled in form of text snippets and uncommented URLs into the Twitter community.

Acknowledgements. The author(s) disclosed receipt of the following financial support for the research, authorship, and/or publication of this article: This project has received funding from the European Union's Horizon 2020 research and innovation programme under the Marie Skłodowska-Curie grant agreement No 823866.

We want to thank Jana Goldau, Melina Baßfeld, and Kaan Eyilmez for their support during the coding process for identifying frames.

8   Appendix

Appendix

Table 1. Summary of the original codebook and the described frame cues by Boydstun et al. [13] and the case specific additions to the codebook including keywords and phrases

Frame dimension	Relevance for case study	Relevant keywords and phrases
Economic	The costs, benefits, or any financial implications of the issue (to an individual, family, organization, community or to the economy as a whole). Impact on Norwegian companies worldwide. E.g. Telenor, one of the major mobile companies in Pakistan, faced reputational damage and customer loss.	Telenor, Pakistan, #boycottNorge
Capacity & Resources	The lack of—or availability of—time, physical, geographical, space, human, and financial resources, or the capacity of existing systems and resources to implement or carry out policy goals. Discussions about limited HR resources of the police to prevent the escalation during the Quran Burning incident. Discussions about the Quran Burning incident focusing on inability of the government due to missing financial or human resources to monitor extremist movements.	lack of police, lack of money, lack of investment
Morality & Ethics	Any perspective that is compelled by religious doctrine or interpretation, duty, honor, righteousness or any other sense of ethics or social or personal responsibility (religious or secular). As the Quran is a religious book and Muslims are a religious community, there are several articles, which contain morality frame cues. Furthermore, the incident triggered discussions about freedom of speech vs. hate speech, which can both be a morality or legality discussion. As well nationalist narratives that the Western culture needs to be protected etc. might fall under this frame.	Religion, Quran, Allah, Freedom of Speech

continued

Table 1. continued

Fairness & Equality	The fairness, equality or inequality with which laws, punishment, rewards, and resources are applied or distributed among individuals or groups. Also the balance between the rights or interests of one individual or group compared to another individual or group As the Muslim community is a minority group in the Norwegian society the fairness and equality frame might apply.	Discrimination in relation to religion, gender, sexual orientation etc.
Legality, Constitutionality & Jurisdiction	The legal, constitutional, or jurisdictional aspects of an issue, where legal aspects include existing laws and court cases; constitutional aspects include all discussion of constitutional interpretation and/or potential revisions; and jurisdiction includes any discussion of which government body should be in charge of a policy decision and/or the appropriate scope of a body's policy reach Discussions on the legality of the burning of the Quran. Is it forbidden by the constitution? As well the legality to generally burn something on a market square was discussed heavily. Furthermore, the Penal Code paragraph 185 (Hate Speech paragraph), was highly discussed in relation to the Quran Burning incident.	Hate Speech paragraph, (Blasphemy) paragraph, Penal Code
Crime & Punishment (Retribution)	The violation of policies in practice and the consequences—retribution—of these violations. As a consequence of the event, seven people were indicted. Three for nuisance, two for violence against the police, and two investigation cases. Even though the incident was potentially legal, it caused law-breaking actions.	punishment, fine, conviction, crime

continued

Table 1. continued

Security & Defense	Any threat to a person, group, or nation, or any defense that needs to be taken to avoid that threat. There have been calls for revenge. The Norwegian flag was burned in Karachi, Pakistan, as a protest. Threats towards Norway have been announced, and people were worried about potential terrorist responses to the incident.	revenge, terrorism, terrorist threat
Health & Safety	The potential health and safety issues. During the protests some people got attacked. If they were physically attacked they felt that their safety and health was at risk.	beaten, hit
Quality of Life	The benefits and costs of any policy on quality of life. The incident has caused fear for revenge. Living in fear and being afraid of new violent situations to occur can have an impact on quality of life.	fear of revenge and violence
Cultural Identity	The social norms, trends, values and customs constituting any culture(s), as they relate to a specific policy issue. Discussions about the struggles of muslim immigrants to find their place in Norway and constant reminders that Norway is not their country of origin and home. Racist and nationalist narratives that people from different countries and cultural backgrounds should not mingle to protect the Western culture and the Western value system.	diaspora, not feeling at home, feeling unaccepted

continued

Table 1. continued

Public Sentiment	The public's opinion. Includes references to general social attitudes, protests, polling and demographic information, as well as implied or actual consequences of diverging from or "getting ahead of" public opinion or polls. The public sentiment plays a role regarding the Quran burning incident e.g. in the form of discussions about the public impression that Norway might not be safe anymore. But as well all stories about certain interest groups (nationalist groups and left-wing groups, minority groups or organizations) can deliver information about the public sentiment in Norway during that time.	Public opinion polls revealed, The majority of the Norwegians
Political Factors & Implications	Any political considerations surrounding an issue. There have been a lot of comments after the event which underlined a political motivation. The right-wing side argued for the idea of Muslims not respecting the values of a western society. The left argued that these kinds of provocations and the right-wings reaction to the situation was done to promote the idea of Muslims being a problem and a threat to society. Both people and politicians used the burning of the Quran to voice political views.	The political party Fremskrittspartiet (FRP) and any other party in Norway and elsewhere, names of politicians
Policy Description, Prescription & Evaluation	Existing policies, policies proposed for addressing an identified problem, as well as analysis of whether hypothetical policies will work, or existing policies are effective. There are stories, which discuss if the current political strategies on how to integrate immigrants into the Norwegian society are working.	immigration law, mandatory language and integration courses

continued

Table 1. continued

External Regulation & Reputation	In general, Norway's external relations with another nation; the external relations of one Norwegian state with another. The event has received international attention. It led to a press release by e.g. the Turkish government or Pakistani politicians.	Ambassador / Ambassadors names, international relations, reputation of Norway
Other	Any frame cue that does not fit in the first 14 dimensions.	
None	Short messages that did not contain any form of framing, but solely a objective description of the situation	Messages like: The Quran was burned on the market place of Kristiansand by members of SIAN.

Table 2. Overview about the online news media part of the online news media data set classified by ownership, affiliation and additional notes regarding the scope of the medium

State-Owned and Mainstream Media	Ownership	Affiliations	Notes
NRK (**www.nrk.no**)	State-owned, under the Ministry of Culture	Member of the Norwegian Press Organization	Largest media house in Norway, non-commercial and politically independent.
VG (www.vg.no),	Owned by Schibsted	Member of the Norwegian Press Organization	Largest newspaper in Norway, significant historical circulation.
Dagbladet (**www.dagbladet. no**)	Owned by Aller Media AS	Member of the Norwegian Press Organization	Daily newspaper with a focus on literature and cultural issues.
TV2 (**www.tv2.no**):	Privately owned	Member of the Norwegian Press Organization	Major broadcaster with significant news coverage.
Online and Independent Media			
Filter Nyheter (**filternyheter.no**):	Independent	Member of the Norwegian Press Organization	Focus on investigative journalism and long-read articles.
Utrop (**www.utrop.no**):	Independent	Member of the Norwegian Press Organization	First newspaper and TV for multicultural news in Norway.

continued

Table 2. continued

Fritanke (fritanke.no):	Independent, associated with the Human-Ethical Association	Adheres to the editor's poster	Focuses on humanist and ethical issues.
Document.no (www.document.no):	Independent	Not a member of the Norwegian Press Organization	Conservative focus, covering major political and social issues.
Resett (resett.no):	Independent	Not a member of the Norwegian Press Organization	Right-wing, focuses on alternative news and opinions. The site has been taken down and is continued under a different name: inyheter.no
Rights.no (www.rights.no):	Human Rights Service (HRS)	Not a member of the Norwegian Press Organization	Focuses on immigration and integration issues, controversial for its stance on Islam.
Gjenstridig.no (www.gjenstridig.no):	Supported by Fritt Ord	Not a member of the Norwegian Press Organization	National conservative, critical of mainstream media.
Lykten.no (www.lykten.no):	Independent	Not a member of the Norwegian Press Organization	Focuses on challenging established media narratives, right-wing orientation.
KSU.no (www.ksu.no)	Independent	Not a member of the Norwegian Press Organization	Focuses on local news in Kristiansund and Nordmøre.

continued

Table 2. continued

Ekte Nyheter (ektenyheter.no):	Independent	Not a member of the Norwegian Press Organization	Minimalist state, libertarian focus, skeptical of mainstream media.
Special Interest and Non-News Platforms			
Imamen.no (imamen.no):	Ahmadiyya Muslim Community	Not a member of the Norwegian Press Organization	Platform for Ahmadiyya imams to present views and engage with the public.
SIAN (www.sian.no):	Stop Islamization of Norway	Not a member of the Norwegian Press Organization	Opposes Islamization, promotes dissemination of information about Islam.
Oppror.net (www.opprop.net):	Independent	Not a news outlet	Platform for creating and promoting signature campaigns.

Table 3. Usage of primary frames and secondary frames in online news sources, tweets, YouTube videos, and YouTube comments. Total numbers in the URL analysis might differ, due to more than one URL per tweet, post or article.

	online news sources		tweets	YouTube videos	YouTube comments
Frame dimension	Count Primary	Count Secondary	Count Primary	Count Primary	Count Primary
Economic	2 (1.8%)	4 (8.0%)	41 (3.6%)	1 (1.4%)	0 (0.0%)
Capacity & Resources	0 (0.0%)	0 (0.0%)	2 (0.2%)	0 (0.0%)	0 (0.0%)
Morality & Ethics	6 (5.5%)	9 (18.0%)	319 (28.1%)	26 (36.6%)	332 (16.3%)
Fairness & Equality	1 (0.9%)	0 (0.0%)	28 (2.5%)	1 (1.4%)	0 (0.0%)
Legality, Constitutionalit y & Jurisdiction	50 (45.9%)	16 (32.0%)	154 (13.6%)	1 (1.4%)	22 (1.1%)
Crime & Punishment	3 (2.8%)	3 (6.0%)	28 (2.5%)	2 (2.8%)	0 (0.0%)
Security & Defense	11 (10.1%)	7 (14.0%)	55 (4.8%)	0 (0.0%)	1 (0.0%)
Health & Safety	1 (0.9%)	0 (0.0%)	42 (3.7%)	0 (0.0%)	0 (0.0%)
Quality of Life	1 (0.9%)	0 (0.0%)	23 (2.0%)	1 (1.4%)	0 (0.0%)
Cultural Identity	1 (0.9%)	0 (0.0%)	48 (4.2%)	0 (0.0%)	0 (0.0%)
Public Sentiment	5 (4.6%)	1 (2.0%)	37 (3.3%)	0 (0.0%)	2 (0.1%)

continued

Table 3. continued

Political Factors & Implications	*10 (9.2%)*	*8 (16.0%)*	*218 (19.2%)*	*1 (1.4%)*	*0 (0.0%)*
Policy Description, Prescription & Evaluation	*4 (3.7%)*	*0 (0.0%)*	*22 (1.9%)*	*0 (0.0%)*	*0 (0.0%)*
External Regulation & Reputation	*13 (11.9 %)*	*2 (4.0%)*	*83 (7.3%)*	*7 (9.9%)*	*106 (5.2%)*
Other	*1 (0.9%)*	*0 (0.0%)*	*3 (0.2%)*	*1 (1.4%)*	*334 (16.4%)*
None	*0 (0.0%)*	*0 (0.0%)*	*33 (2.9%)*	*30 (42.3%)*	*558 (27.4%)*
Sum	***109 (100%)***	***50 (100%)***	***1136 (100%)***	***71 (100%)***	***2031 (100%)***

Table 4. Cohen's Kappa Coefficient per medium and its interpretation

Medium	Cohen's Kappa Coefficient	Interpretation according to Landis and Koch (1977)
Twitter	0.86	Almost perfect
YouTube videos	0.89	Almost perfect
YouTube comments	0.87	Almost perfect
Newspaper articles	0.87	Almost perfect

References

1. Bruns, A.: Gatewatching and News Curation: Journalism, Social Media, and the Public Sphere (Digital Formations, Volume 113). Peter Lang Publishing, Lausanne (2018)
2. Entman, R.M.: Framing: toward clarification of a fractured paradigm. J. Commun. **43**(4), 51–58 (1993)
3. Jung, A.K., Mirbabaie, M., Ross, B., Stieglitz, S., Neuberger, C., Kapidzic, S.: Information diffusion between twitter and online media (2018)
4. Hasan, H., Hashim, L.: What's new in online news. In: PACIS 2009 Proceedings, p. 42 (2009)
5. Bateson, G.: A Theory of Play and Fantasy. MIT Press, Boston (1972)
6. Goffman, E.: Frame Analysis: An Essay on the Organization of Experience. Harvard University Press, Cambridge (1974)
7. Schaffner, B.F., Sellers, P.J.: Winning with words. In: The Origins and Impact of Political Framing, New York, London (2010)
8. Orlikowski, W.J., Gash, D.C.: Technological frames: making sense of information technology in organizations. ACM Trans. Inf. Syst. (TOIS) **12**(2), 174–207 (1994)
9. Touri, M., Koteyko, N.: Using corpus linguistic software in the extraction of news frames: towards a dynamic process of frame analysis in journalistic texts. Int. J. Soc. Res. Methodol. **18**(6), 601–616 (2015)
10. Matthes, J., Kohring, M.: The content analysis of media frames: toward improving reliability and validity. J. Commun. **58**(2), 258–279 (2008)
11. Van Gorp, B., Vercruysse, T.: Frames and counter-frames giving meaning to dementia: a framing analysis of media content. Soc. Sci. Med. **74**(8), 1274–1281 (2012)
12. Boydstun, A.E., Card, D., Gross, J.H., Resnik, P., Smith, N.A.: Tracking the development of media frames within and across policy issues. In: APSA 2014 Annual Meeting Paper (2014)
13. Card, D., Boydstun, A., Gross, J.H., Resnik, P., Smith, N.A.: The media frames corpus: annotations of frames across issues. In: Proceedings of the 53rd Annual Meeting of the Association for Computational Linguistics and the 7th International Joint Conference on Natural Language Processing (Volume 2: Short Papers), pp. 438–444 (2015)
14. Chadwick, A., Dennis, J., Smith, A.P.: Politics in the age of hybrid media: power, systems, and media logics. In: The Routledge Companion to Social Media and Politics, pp. 7–22. Routledge, London (2015)
15. Meraz, S., Papacharissi, Z.: Networked gatekeeping and networked framing on# Egypt. Int. J. Press/Polit. **18**(2), 138–166 (2013)
16. Kermani, H., Adham, M.: Mapping Persian Twitter: networks and mechanism of political communication in Iranian 2017 presidential election. Big Data Soc. **8**(1), 20539517211025570 (2021)
17. Walsh, J.P.: Digital nativism: Twitter, migration discourse and the 2019 election. New Media Soc. **25**(10), 2618–2643 (2023)
18. Knüpfer, C., Hoffmann, M., Voskresenskii, V.: Hijacking metoo: transnational dynamics and networked frame contestation on the far right in the case of the '120 decibels' campaign. Inf. Commun. Soc. **25**(7), 1010–1028 (2022)
19. Pöyhtäri, R., Nelimarkka, M., Nikunen, K., Ojala, M., Pantti, M., Pääkkönen, J.: Refugee debate and networked framing in the hybrid media environment. Int. Commun. Gaz. **83**(1), 81–102 (2021)

20. Zafarani, R., Abbasi, M.A., Liu, H.: Social Media Mining: An Introduction. Cambridge University Press, Cambridge (2014)
21. Shahi, G.K., Dirkson, A., Majchrzak, T.A.: An exploratory study of COVID-19 misinformation on Twitter. Online So. Netw. Media **22**, 100104 (2021)
22. Shahi, G.K., Kana Tsoplefack, W.: Mitigating harmful content on social media using an interactive user interface. In: Hopfgartner, F., Jaidka, K., Mayr, P., Jose, J., Breitsohl, J. (eds.) SocInfo 2022. LNCS, vol. 13618, pp. 490–505. Springer, Cham (2022). https://doi.org/10.1007/978-3-031-19097-1_34
23. Liu, L., Wang, X., Zheng, Y., Fang, W., Tang, S., Zheng, Z.: Homogeneity trend on social networks changes evolutionary advantage in competitive information diffusion. New J. Phys. **22**(1), 013019 (2020)
24. Syn, S.Y., Oh, S.: Why do social network site users share information on Facebook and Twitter? J. Inf. Sci. **41**(5), 553–569 (2015)
25. Su, C., Guan, X., Du, Y., Huang, X., Zhang, M.: Toward capturing heterogeneity for inferring diffusion networks: a mixed diffusion pattern model. Knowl.-Based Syst. **147**, 81–93 (2018)
26. Sela, A., Goldenberg, D., Ben-Gal, I., Shmueli, E.: Active viral marketing: incorporating continuous active seeding efforts into the diffusion model. Expert Syst. Appl. **107**, 45–60 (2018)
27. Hosseini-Pozveh, M., Zamanifar, K., Naghsh-Nilchi, A.R.: Assessing information diffusion models for influence maximization in signed social networks. Expert Syst. Appl. **119**, 476–490 (2019)
28. Molaei, S., Zare, H., Veisi, H.: Deep learning approach on information diffusion in heterogeneous networks. Knowl.-Based Syst. **189**, 105153 (2020)
29. Han, Y., Lappas, T., Sabnis, G.: The importance of interactions between content characteristics and creator characteristics for studying virality in social media. Inf. Syst. Res. **31**(2), 576–588 (2020)
30. Probst, F., Grosswiele, L., Pfleger, R.: Who will lead and who will follow: identifying influential users in online social networks: a critical review and future research directions. Wirtschaftsinformatik **55**, 175–192 (2013)
31. Wang, Z., Liu, H., Liu, W., Wang, S.: Understanding the power of opinion leaders' influence on the diffusion process of popular mobile games: travel frog on Sina Weibo. Comput. Hum. Behav. **109**, 106354 (2020)
32. Mirbabaie, M., Bunker, D., Stieglitz, S., Marx, J., Ehnis, C.: Social media in times of crisis: learning from hurricane Harvey for the coronavirus disease 2019 pandemic response. J. Inf. Technol. **35**(3), 195–213 (2020)
33. Stieglitz, S., Dang-Xuan, L.: Emotions and information diffusion in social media-sentiment of microblogs and sharing behavior. J. Manag. Inf. Syst. **29**(4), 217–248 (2013)
34. Kane, G.C., Alavi, M., Labianca, G., Borgatti, S.P.: What's different about social media networks? A framework and research agenda. MIS Q. **38**(1), 275–304 (2014)
35. Krijestorac, H., Garg, R., Mahajan, V.: Cross-platform spillover effects in consumption of viral content: a quasi-experimental analysis using synthetic controls. Inf. Syst. Res. **31**(2), 449–472 (2020)
36. Myers, S.A., Zhu, C., Leskovec, J.: Information diffusion and external influence in networks. In: Proceedings of the 18th ACM SIGKDD International Conference on Knowledge Discovery and Data Mining, pp. 33–41 (2012)
37. Mathes, R., Pfetsch, B.: The role of the alternative press in the agenda-building process: spill-over effects and media opinion leadership. Eur. J. Commun. **6**(1), 33–62 (1991)

38. Pfetsch, B., Adam, S., Lance Bennett, W.: The critical linkage between online and offline media: an approach to researching the conditions of issue spill-over. Javnost-Publ. **20**(3), 9–22 (2013)
39. Shahi, G.K., Nandini, D.: Fakecovid–a multilingual cross-domain fact check news dataset for COVID-19 (2020). https://workshop-proceedings.icwsm.org/abstract.php?id=2020_14
40. Stahl, B.C.: Morality, ethics, and reflection: a categorization of normative is research. J. Assoc. Inf. Syst. **13**(8), 1 (2012)
41. Kekes, J.: Moral intuition. Am. Philos. Q. **23**(1), 83–93 (1986)
42. Starbird, K.: Facts, frames, and (mis)interpretations: understanding rumors as collective sensemaking. https://www.cip.uw.edu/2023/12/06/rumors-collective-sensemaking-kate-starbird/. Accessed 11 July 2024
43. Alkiviadou, N.: Hate speech on social media networks: towards a regulatory framework? Inf. Commun. Technol. Law **28**(1), 19–35 (2019)
44. Lim, H., Fussell, S.R.: Making sense of foreign language posts in social media. Proc. ACM Hum.-Comput. Interact. **1**(CSCW), 1–16 (2017)

Understanding Political Communication and Polarisation: A Case Study of the Colombian President's X Utilisation

María José González-Méndez[(✉)] and Niklas Kloth

Department of Information Systems, University of Münster, Leonardo-Campus 3, 48149 Münster, Germany
mariajose.gonzalezmendez@uni-muenster.de

Abstract. The shape of social media platforms has transformed political communication, particularly how political leaders engage with the public and influence opinion. This paper explores the dynamics of Colombian President Gustavo Petro's use of X, formerly known as Twitter, to comprehend the transmission of digital political polarisation through political posts. The study examined two months' worth of posts using a deductive coding method, applying the tactics of *positive self-presentation* and *negative other-presentation* identified by previous research. The analysis revealed a significant use of polarising posts, with 61% of President Petro's posts employing either positive frames, negative ones, or both. These findings provide insight into the techniques used to create political divisions on social media platforms and contribute to ongoing discussions in the field of political communication studies.

Keywords: social science · X · polarisation · Colombia · framing theory · positive self-presentation · negative other-presentation

1 Introduction

The rapid adoption of new digital technologies, such as social media platforms [3], has encouraged political leaders to utilise these channels as a means to engage with citizens or users, serving as a tool for political communication [4]. On that account, social media platforms have become relevant instruments for political leaders to influence public opinion and establish agendas [5]. X, formerly known as Twitter, particularly, has emerged as a favourite social media tool among political leaders globally [6], due to its ability to provide instant communication and a wide audience reach that surpasses traditional media channels [7].

While these platforms can facilitate social connection and cohesion, they can also have the opposite effect if politicians support views that generate division among people [4]. For instance, when it comes to a sensitive topic like migration, spreading divisive views can worsen societal tensions towards immigrant communities, preventing productive discussions, and intensifying pre-existing differences. Therefore, the use of social

M. Preuss et al. (Eds.): MISDOOM 2024, LNCS 15175, pp. 131–145, 2024.
https://doi.org/10.1007/978-3-031-71210-4_8

media by public figures has not only promoted connectedness but also generated concerns about its ability to worsen disinformation, hate speech, and societal polarisation [8]. Recent research [9] discusses the potential long-term effects on the functioning and credibility of democratic processes, highlighting the crucial role of information and shared narratives in fostering high-quality democratic public discourse [10].

Gustavo Petro, President of Colombia 2022–2026, exemplifies how political leaders can strategically employ X to shape public discourse and wield influence. The extensive utilisation of the platform by Petro has generated significant attention, which earned him the title of "Twittering President" from the Colombian press [11, 12] and recognition as the 4th most influential leader on X in 2022 [13], underscoring the strength of his social media account (@petrogustavo) and consequently the importance of it in his contemporary political communication. Social media platforms offer political leaders an ideal setting to mobilise support, get people to back them, advocate for the sovereignty of the people, and criticise the establishments of power [14]. Unlike traditional communication channels, social media platforms use algorithms to prioritise engagement, which frequently results in the amplification of emotionally charged or controversial information [15]. This algorithmic design encourages the sharing of content that generates strong reactions, such as hostility and outrage. Hence, leaders who are skilled at producing controversial messages can use this algorithmic inclination to gain attention and gather support [14].

Consequently, there has been a growing interest in examining political messages on social media platforms and analysing how the messages are shaped [16]. Particularly, this paper wants to identify the presence of polarisation frames in President Gustavo Petro's posts on X. Understanding that polarisation frames are a rhetorical and communicative strategy used in political discourse to create a clear division between an in-group and an out-group. This leads to the following research question:

Does President Gustavo Petro's utilisation of X exhibit indications of polarisation in his political communication? If that is the case, how?

To answer the research question, a total of two months' worth of the subject's X account were gathered manually and subsequently, two iterations of qualitative content analysis were applied, following a deductive coding approach. This approach has proven valuable in previous research and draws on framing theory and political communication [1, 2].

2   Research Background

2.1   Framing Theory

From the areas of psychology and communication, framing theory has evolved as a paradigm for understanding how information is constructed, disseminated, and received in society [17–19]. For scholars, news is presented in a certain way to offer an explanation about who is doing what and for what purpose, but that narrative excludes parts of the events [20–22]. Particularly, Tuchman [21] characterised the news media as a "window to the world," highlighting how framing choices made by journalists and media organisations shape the information landscape by selectively emphasising certain aspects of events while downplaying or excluding others. For example, the view from a window depends on whether it is large or small, or whether its glass is clear or opaque. In other words, limiting the view of reality focuses attention on a specific fragment.

Entman [22] further argued that "frame information" involves selecting certain aspects of reality, giving them more relevance in a communicative text, and, by doing so, delivering an intended interpretation, moral evaluation, or recommendation for assessing the information provided [23]. Therefore, framing acknowledges a text's ability to define a situation or issue and establish the terms of the debate [24]. As a result, there are four key areas where framing can occur: in the communicator, the text, the receiver, and the culture, which stress the complex nature of framing processes within the communication ecosystem. From the deliberate framing choices made by communicators to the interpretive frames employed by audiences, framing operates at multiple levels, influencing both the production and reception of mediated messages.

Subsequently, framing is not merely a static process but rather a dynamic one that encompasses the creation—frame building—, selection and presentation—frame setting—, and establishment of certain frames—frame effects— [25]. Thus, a study can focus on the entire process or on the frames within the different stages through which it passes. The current study focused on the second stage, the frame setting located in the text available to the public, in this case, posts on the social media platform X. The text's frames manifest through the presence or absence of certain keywords, stereotyped images, information sources, and sentences containing judgements that thematically reinforce the content. To establish the presence or absence of frames, the concepts and stereotypical images that can indicate political polarisation will be presented next.

2.2 Polarisation Framework

In political communication, the eloquence of political discourse has invited researchers to analyse the widely used strategies of rhetoric and persuasion of politicians in their speeches [26, 27]. One of the most remarkable patterns of political discourse is the polarisation strategy of "us" and "them," marked by the binary propositions of *positive self-presentation* and *negative other-presentation* [1, 2, 27, 28].

According to Masroor et al. [1], there are new emerging forms of polarisation in political discourse via political posts, extending the general themes of *positive self-presentation* and *negative other-presentation* of van Dijk [2]. As a result, the authors identified sub themes within these binary categories to understand how politicians use them in their posts to represent their ideological presence online.

On the one hand, there is the concept of *negative other-presentation*, in which political actors attempt to harm the reputation of the out-group or opposing parties in the eyes of the public [1]. The frame incorporates a variety of tactics for delegitimizing the *other* to diminish their legitimacy and influence. The ways of representing the *other* can be as follows: (i) disloyal to the country; (ii) lacking credibility; (iii) looter; (iv) criminal; (v) proven guilty of a crime; (vi) oppressor; and (vi) lacking rationality.

On the other hand, Masroor's et al. [1] framework also explores the theme of *positive self-presentation*, wherein political actors seek to bolster their own image and credibility. They may emphasise qualities such as being hard-working, loyal, brave, and essential for the nation's well-being. These strategies include portraying oneself as: (i) a personification of goodness; (ii) the only hope for the nation; and (iii) one with the nation.

Overall, Masroor's et al. [1] framework offers a comprehensive lens through which it is possible to look at some of the dynamics of polarisation within the larger context of political communication. This theory helps to understand how polarisation works in modern digital political discourse by identifying some of the techniques used by political players to affect public perceptions and further their own goals against their opposition.

2.3 Related Work

Multiple studies have conducted an analysis of the messages disseminated by politicians and their public rhetorical leadership as a means of exercising influence [16, 29–36]. In general, the objectives have been to investigate the presence of any underlying empirical tendencies in politicians' use of social media platforms, mainly X, across different countries and periods of time, particularly during elections [37, 38]. The use of diverse coding techniques in nearly all studies makes direct comparisons between them difficult. However, certain consistent findings about politicians' use of X appear to be present in some of the research [16].

For instance, across election cycles in various countries, politicians often leverage X as their primary platform to share campaign details, policy statements, and links to personal websites, with fewer instances of direct appeals for voter turnout or donations. Furthermore, interactions with other users on X are sporadic, predominantly centred on engagement with fellow politicians or journalists [29].

Further research reveals that there is strong evidence of increasingly polarising public opinions on social media platforms such as X [30]. Studies have elucidated deliberate strategies by political leaders, particularly right-wing parties, to promote their agendas and polarise discourse on social media platforms [31]. In this case, political leaders' unidirectional use of X and high user response rates exacerbate the polarisation [32]. Additionally, some studies indicated that political homophily, the tendency for people to form ties with those who are similar, facilitates the sharing of political attitudes, contributing to political polarisation [33].

Moreover, studies about the Latin American presidential elections have examined emotions and their relationship to polarisation within digital communities, revealing an evolving emotional tone of posts, formerly known as tweets, over time, along with an increase in digital polarisation [39]. This highlights the key link between communication ties and political polarisation, which is critical for understanding the dynamics of liberal democracies, as well as the importance of fostering public discourse that includes a variety of ideas and interests [30].

Finally, other studies have viewed populism as a distinctive style of political communication, characterised by elements such as top-down, leader-centred communication, antagonistic discourse against critics (including journalists and the media), and a fixation with news coverage [36]. Findings have concluded that social media provides a platform that emphasises affect and personality, two essential elements of populist-style rhetoric, a term frequently associated with politicians beyond the political establishment [35].

Overall, research on political communication through social media platforms has contributed to the understanding that these platforms can either enclose politicians in echo chambers or open up cross-ideological and cross-party interactions, thereby impacting the public sphere in online legislative networks [33].

3 Research Method

3.1 Research Design

The study adopted an exploratory-descriptive approach through a qualitative content analysis methodology, allowing for the extraction of quantifiable information from President Gustavo Petro's posts, by employing variables to expose polarisation frames within his political communication [40]. According to Krippendorff [41], content analysis involves rigorously and systematically studying the nature of messages exchanged in communication acts. It is a research technique aimed at formulating reproducible and valid inferences from certain data that can be applied to their context.

A deductive method was used for the frame-setting analysis, which aligned with Masroor et al.'s framework [1]. Given the ample amount of existing research on the nature and mechanisms of polarisation [26], a deductive method was seen fit to build on established conceptual frameworks and discover predefined defining features of the polarisation frame. This technique not only speeds the analytic process, but it also ensures that the study's conclusions are consistent with earlier scholarship, allowing comparability and boosting their validity.

3.2 Data

For this study, two months of posts from President Petro's first year in government were chosen: March and June 2023. The rationale for this period of data collection emerged, on the one hand, being the two months in which Gustavo Petro most posted on X— between original posts, quote posts, post replies, and reposts—being 771 posts in March and 683 in June, according to a study from news outlet El Espectador and independent non-profit organisation Linterna Verde [42]. On top of that, the months were chosen to explore the day-to-day politics and administration of President Petro's agenda without the influence of campaign dynamics or other specific events, which could alter the daily polarisation dissemination due to the implied spikes caused by the competitive political context of those scenarios. Moreover, by studying posts from numerous months, the study identifies trends and fluctuations in President Petro's communication over time, thereby increasing the robustness of the results.

However, the study only concentrated on original posts, quote posts, and post replies authored by President Petro or in which he responded to others. The reposts were not included in the analysis since they do not reflect the president's direct writing, and the purpose of the analysis is to identify any signs of polarisation by examining the presence of *positive self-presentation* and *negative other-presentation* in the content of each post written by Petro.

The data was collected manually in March 2024 by utilising the Advanced Search feature in X. The postings from President Petro's account (@petrogustavo) were filtered by time, selecting the two months stated above.

Table 1. Polarisation frames questions.

Negative Other-Presentation		0	1
Disloyal to the Country	Is it stated or implied in the text that the "other" does not represent democracy in its purest form because it does not act in the public interest?	No	Yes
Lacks Credibility	Is the text stating or implying that the "other" is a dishonest and immoral person? Does the text explicitly state that the "other" tells "lies" and "allegations"?	No	Yes
Is a Looter	Does the text discredit the "other" and prove it wrong using numerical games, "hard facts," and direct quotes?	No	Yes
Is a Criminal	Does the text assert or suggest that any wrongdoing is the result of the "other's" criminal mindset? Is the "other" presented as "criminals" and labelled as such?	No	Yes
Is Proven Guilty	Does the text describe or cite a decision given by some authority against the "other" for his or her criminal actions?	No	Yes
Is an Oppressor	Does the text portray the "other" as an oppressor or tyrant incapable of engaging in constructive debate and determined to impose their beliefs on others by any means necessary?	No	Yes
Lacks Rationality	Does the text assert or imply that the "other" is deranged or insane? Does the text use irony and sarcasm to verbally attack the "other"?	No	Yes
Positive Self-Presentation		0	1
Personification of Goodness	Does the text characterise the "self" as hardworking, efficient, courageous, honest, trustworthy, loyal, and/or resilient? Is there an endowment of self-glorification and good self-presentation to its party and others who belong to its group with "facts"?	No	Yes
Only Hope for the Nation	Does the text portray the "self," or its political party, as the last hope for the country?	No	Yes
One With the Nation	Does the text assert or suggest that the "self's" victory equals the nation's glory and success, and that what is beneficial to oneself also benefits the nation? Is the text an invitation or an offer to "join us"?	No	Yes

3.3 Analysis

To meet the research objective, each post collected was identified using location variables, such as: (i) date of post, (ii) publication time, (iii) edition of the post, (iv) type of post, (v) content, (vi) link within the post, (vii) source of the quoted post or link, (viii) main topic, (ix) impressions, (x) replies, (xi) reposts, and (xii) likes. Numerical values were assigned, representing specific attributes of the posts, to these location variables. The posts' main topic was coded to identify which subjects are most relevant to President Gustavo Petro. The topic selection, unlike the polarisation frameworks, was done inductively, given that the categories were created as the posts were analysed.

The topics were identified and categorised based on emerging patterns within the data, ensuring that each category created, although broad, was mutually exclusive and exhaustive compared to the other ones. For instance, there were various posts that discussed the bill proposals that Petro's government wanted to implement, ranging from health, education, agriculture, etc., but they all fell under the category of 'bill proposals' because the focus was on the legislative process rather than the content of the bill itself. Furthermore, the researchers independently coded the data to ensure reliability. Hence, there was a comparison of the coding results to identify discrepancies and achieve consensus on the topic categories.

Once the units of analysis were identified, the frames were evaluated based on questions that referred to the absence or presence of each frame outlined in the theoretical framework. The coding questions were constructed using Masroor's work, operationalizing their findings into a set of questions suitable for online posting analysis. Table 1 displays all the polarisation frames questions. Each of Petro's posts was then categorised based on the 10 main aspects of polarisation frames. These questions aided the research in minimising personal bias during the coding process, and they can also serve as a valuable resource for future researchers looking at social media platforms for political purposes. Moreover, to reduce any possible contextual bias, it is important to note that the second author had no previous knowledge or familiarity with Gustavo Petro, the President of Colombia.

4 Results

4.1 Preliminary Analysis

As mentioned, the two months in which Gustavo Petro most posted on X in his first year as president were March (771) and June (682), between original posts, quote posts, post replies, and reposts. However, this study exclusively examined the original posts, quote posts, and post replies from those two months, excluding any reposts not authored by Petro. As a result, the research covered a total of 510 posts, quote posts, and post replies by Gustavo Petro, published in March 2023 and June 2023. Out of these, 315 were from March, and 195 fell in June. Original posts were the most popular type of post in both March (130) and June (96), followed by quote posts (212) and post replies (72).

During the two months, President Petro published most posts between 08:00 and 11:59 (163 posts) and between 16:00 and 19:59 (109 posts). Moreover, only a small fraction (1.2%) of Petro's posts have been updated after being published. Generally, even if there are typographical errors in the post, they are not corrected once published.

In terms of post content, there was a diverse range. The most common type of post was a text that included a quoted post, accounting for 41.8% of the total. Posts with both text and an image came next, accounting for 29.2% of the total. Lastly, there were posts that consisted solely of text, which accounted for 24.5%. A mere 2.9% of posts had solely an image or a video. These specific postings were excluded from the frame analysis because the study focused exclusively on text framing. As a result, the research sample employed a total of 495 posts to analyse the polarisation frames.

The examination of engagement analytics uncovers significant trends in the audience's response to President Gustavo Petro's messages on X. In terms of impressions, more than half of the posts, comprising 58.6%, obtained views ranging from 0 to 499,999. Another 24.1% of posts fell within the range of 500,000 to 999,999 views. Surprisingly, 17.2% of posts received considerably more views, ranging from 1,200,000 to 7,500,000, demonstrating a considerable influence on the number of people reached and the level of visibility.

Replies, reposts, and likes follow the same pattern. A large proportion of posts were in the lower ranges for all three metrics. Most posts received a small number of responses, with an average of 1411 replies. Similarly, many posts had a low number of shares or reposts, usually ranging from 0 to 2999 reposts. Finally, in terms of likes, most posts received an average of 8500. Conversely, an even more modest yet significant proportion of posts, 4.1%, generated a greater degree of audience participation, suggesting lively discourse, amplification, and support. These statistics emphasise the many levels of audience connection and showcase the effectiveness of specific posts in generating meaningful conversation on the site.

Furthermore, President Gustavo Petro's posts addressed a wide range of issues, reflecting the complexities of the public conversation. The majority of his posts focused on matters of national importance. Among the main topics, the economy was the dominant emphasis, accounting for 9.9% of posts, followed by regions (8.7%), media outlets and journalists (8.2%), bill proposals (7.7%), and protest marches (6%).

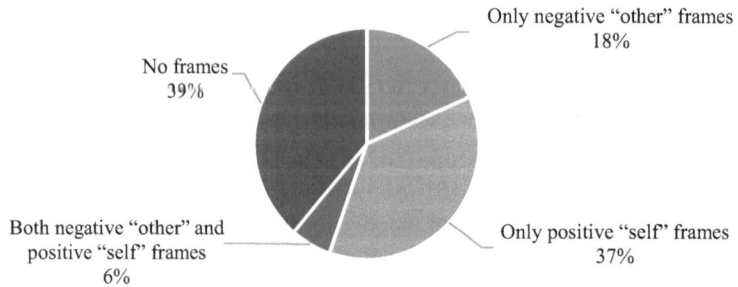

Fig. 1. Polarisation frames results.

4.2 Petro's Polarisation Frames

Out of the 495 posts that were examined—image and video posts were excluded from the text framing analysis—, 39% were found to be **neutral**, with no polarisation frame identified. Yet the examination of polarisation frames in Petro's posts also revealed a significant occurrence of both negative and positive framing tactics, accounting for 61%. The distribution of the discovered polarisation frames is illustrated in Fig. 1.

37% of the posts on X, which is equivalent to 183 posts, employed exclusively **positive frames**, depicting President Petro in a favourable manner. Within this positive self-presentation, *Personification of Goodness* (82%), which portrays President Petro as embodying virtuous qualities, and *One with the Nation* (31.1%), which highlights his alignment with the nation's interests and aspirations, were the most used positive frames. The frame of *Only Hope for the Nation* was not significant (0.5%), with only 1 post assigned out of the 183.

> "For a century, Timbiquí, Cauca, waited in the face of indolent governments. In the government of change, its aqueduct and drinking water for its boys and girls are facts." – Post N.°368

> "The Brazilian press cites as an example the tax reform we managed to get through." – Post N.°370

The first post aligns with the category of *Personification of Goodness* as it portrays President Petro as an agent of positive change and benevolence. By highlighting the provision of essential services, like an aqueduct, the post characterises President Petro and the "government of change" as efficient and trustworthy, thus self-glorifying and presenting a positive image of oneself and his administration. Similarly, the second post corresponds to the category of *One with the Nation* by linking personal achievements with national success. By attributing the approval of the tax reform to himself and his administration, President Petro presents his victories as synonymous with the progress and prosperity of the nation, thereby positioning himself as integral to the nation's success and aligning his personal wins with national accomplishments.

In contrast, 91 posts, constituting 18% of the sample, employed **exclusively negative frames**, focusing on portraying others, typically political opponents, or media outlet critics, in a negative way. In this category, the most commonly used negative frames were *Looter* (51.6%), *Lacks Credibility* (33%), *Disloyal to the Country* (27.5%), and *Criminal* (20.9%), used to undermine the credibility and integrity of perceived adversaries. The frames of *Oppressor* (9.9%), *Lacks Rationality* (5.5%), and *Proven Guilty* (2.2.%) were also used but in a reduced number of posts, serving to reinforce President Petro's own image while casting doubt or criticism on others within the political sphere.

> "The prosecutor criticises Mazzucato's thesis on the importance of public contracting with communal and popular actions. This is the way to democratise the economy. Haven't they ever tired of fattening big contracting cartels?" – Post N.°62

> "What nonsense that they destroy the possibility of defending society against telematic attacks. I guess Uribe Turbay doesn't know what that is." – Post N.°58

Post N.°62 falls into the category of *Disloyal to the Country* due to its portrayal of the prosecutor as undermining efforts to democratise the economy and combat corruption. The post, which implies that the prosecutor's activities help large contracting cartels, demonstrates betrayal of the country's welfare. Similarly, the second post falls into the category of being *Disloyal to the Country* and *Lacks Rationality* by doubting Uribe Turbay's competency and motives in addressing cybersecurity threats. By dismissing Uribe Turbay's actions as nonsensical and implying ignorance, the post undermines his opponent's image, demeaning him and encouraging the audience not to believe what he says.

Interestingly, a smaller subset of 29 posts, representing 6% of the sample, employed both **negative and positive frames simultaneously**. This approach suggests a strategic use of framing techniques to simultaneously enhance Petro's image while discrediting opponents. Within this scenario, for instance, the posts combine positive self-framing, such as *Personification of Goodness* (89.7%), with negative other-framing, such as *Looter* (41.4%), *Criminal* (37.9%), and *Disloyal to the Country* (37.9%), to convey a sense of urgency or necessity in supporting the President's agenda.

> "All the armed groups that today create violence were established after the Santos peace process and in the Duque government. No group has been created in my government. We are looking for them to cease their actions." – Post N.°149

> "There is an absolute difference between cybersecurity and illegal wiretapping. Your government, Mr. Uribe Turbay, made illegal wiretapping; my government wants to defend the citizenship of that, which is cybersecurity." – Post N.°54

In the first post, Petro portrays his government as an example of peace and stability by emphasising the lack of armed group creation throughout his time in office. This aligns with the *Personification of Goodness*, portraying the government as committed to peace. However, the post also engages in negative other-framing by blaming prior administrations for the formation of armed organisations, implying a lack of legitimacy and perhaps criminal activity on their behalf. Similarly, Post N.°54 uses *Personification of Goodness* to position Petro's administration as an advocate of cybersecurity and the rule of law. However, it also engages in negative other-framing by accusing his opponent's prior government of unlawful wiretapping, undermining their credibility, and possibly implying criminal activity. This combination of positive self-framing and negative other-framing reinforces the President's image while casting doubt on their opponents.

5   Discussion

The analysis of President Gustavo Petro's post reveals distinct patterns of communication and engagement. The majority of these posts used text with quoted posts, but a notable number also included images. Engagement varied significantly, with a smaller proportion of posts achieving high levels of interaction, which points to a polarised response from the audience. From the analysis of the sample of posts, it was possible to identify a high number of 61% of his posts as polarising, where most of them were solely positive self-presentations, followed by a negative presentation of "the other". This implies that, on average, Petro publishes approximately five polarising posts each day.

The data indicates that President Petro strategically uses X to present a positive image through frames that emphasise his alignment with national interests and his role as a benevolent leader. However, the presence of negative framing towards opponents suggests a deliberate approach to discredit opposition, which might contribute to polarised public perceptions by directly engaging with the public, as his formal role as President means that he receives a great deal of attention, far beyond his own supporters alone. The high engagement on some posts, particularly those that either highly praise or strongly criticise, underscores the polarising nature of the content, overarching the framing theory alone.

5.1 Implications for Research

The results of this study fit into the findings of other research and offer valuable insights into the dynamics of political communication on social media platforms. First and foremost, by being able to apply the frames of Masroor et al. [1] in a successful way. By identifying the frames of political communication, the current literature was enhanced and offered valuable insights into political communication.

Furthermore, the findings align with the related work and feature President Petro's high level of polarisation [16, 29–36]. By demonstrating the presence of polarisation frames in President Petro's posts, we corroborate existing evidence suggesting that social media platforms can exacerbate societal divisions and hinder productive dialogue. The study sheds light on the specific polarisation tactics employed by political leaders, such as *negative other-presentation* and *positive self-presentation*. The identification of these themes provides a nuanced understanding of how political actors construct their online personas and engage with their audiences, offering valuable insights for researchers studying digital political communication.

This study involved a manual evaluation of posts, focusing exclusively on their content without assessing responses or accuracy. Political communication frequently employs implicit methods, implications, and various stylistic devices, making objective evaluation challenging. While this approach successfully identified a significant number of polarising posts, it is important to acknowledge that some posts may not have been categorised as such because they did not align neatly with the predefined categories of the analytical framework. This highlights the inherent complexities and potential limitations of the methodology in capturing the full spectrum of polarising communication.

5.2 Implications for Practice

These findings underline the role of social media as a powerful tool in modern political strategy, where leaders not only communicate policies but also shape their public persona and manage opposition narratives. For President Petro, X as a platform acts as a direct channel to the public, bypassing traditional media filters, which may enhance followers' perceptions of transparency and authenticity.

For practitioners, this study underscores the importance of strategic framing in social media communications. Tailoring messaging to emphasise positive frames that align political figures with national interests as well as negative framing towards opponents has the potential to increase engagement. While framing is successfully used in social media in the presence, negative effects on democracy in the long run should not go unnoticed, as Blassing et al. [14] already discovered. This paper calls attention to their position and could implicate further regulation to protect democracy itself. This, however, might conflict with the monetary driven interest of platforms for users to engage longer with the platform, which is typical for especially polarising posts [15]. Hence, the interest in self-regulating themselves as platforms might be narrow, leaving the responsibility to lawmakers.

However, it is clear to acknowledge that framing and polarisation happen daily in social media platforms. Understanding the mechanisms is therefore crucial in order to react towards polarising posts.

5.3 Limitations

Even though the study analysed almost 500 posts from President Petro, the analysis is limited to two distinct months and does not account for external events that may have influenced the content or reception of the posts. Also, only direct posts were studied, meaning that responses were not included in the analysis. Additionally, the exclusion of posts with only images or videos may omit aspects of the communication strategy.

Therefore, the analysed posts as a sample cannot be generalised directly. Means for generalizability are elaborated in the implications for further research. Although one of the researchers lacked any knowledge of Petro and his posts, in an intentional effort to minimise subjective bias towards the posts, inherent bias persists in the individual analysis of communication. Finally, the analysis did not account for the demographics of the audience engaging with the posts, as X does not represent a whole country.

6 Conclusion

Polarisation on social media in general, but especially on X, is a widely recognised topic in research [37]. Social media is a very useful platform for politicians to directly communicate with a large number of people without news networks filtering the communication [37, 38]. Therefore, political communication is also a widely researched topic in general, as the power behind it can either benefit democracies or degrade them [37, 38]. Manipulation of beliefs and behaviours is therefore an important concern in political research. This is also undermined by the unpredicted results of recent votes, where social media played an important role in success [38]. Implications in current research name polarisation as the exploitation of democratic deficits [37].

The sample of 495 out of Gustavo Petro's 510 posts over two selected months provided significant insights about polarisation. After analysing the posts using the framing theory, it was possible to identify 61% as polarising, whereby the positive self-presentation dominated the polarised posts by far, followed by negatively presenting the "other." Some posts included both a positive self-presentation and a negative attitude towards the "other." In his communication, he focused on topics such as the economy, media outlets, journalists, and protest marches. Hence, the paper showed that the polarisation on social media was exemplary in the case of Gustavo Petro.

The study suggests several aspects for future research. First, extending the analysis period could provide insights into how political communication strategies evolve over time or in response to specific political events. For that, new means of analysis, such as the involvement of large language models (LLM), could also be introduced. The manually evaluated data could be used as a baseline and for verification in order to train an LLM. Using such tools could provide not just an analysis over time, but also a linkage between polarisation and real-world changes. Secondly, comparative studies involving other political figures could reveal whether the framing techniques identified are idiosyncratic to President Petro or widely used across political leaders. In that regard, current research already analyses framing for political leaders, but analysing the real-world impact could be a more fruitful approach [37].

Acknowledgements. This research article received assistance from the Linterna Verde organisation, which shared the post count during the first year of Petro's government.

References

1. Masroor, F., Khan, Q.N., Aib, I., Ali, Z.: Polarization and ideological weaving in Twitter discourse of politicians. Soc. Media Soc. **5**, 205630511989122 (2019)
2. van Dijk, T.A.: Principles of critical discourse analysis. Discourse Soc. **4**, 249–283 (1993)
3. Olsen, N.V., Christensen, K.: Social media, new digital technologies and their potential application in sensory and consumer research. Curr. Opin. Food Sci. **3**, 23–26 (2015)
4. Gómez Céspedes, L.M.: Comunicación política por Twitter. Colombia: a un tuit de la democracia. Universidad Sergio Arboleda, Bogotá (2016)
5. Amado, A., Waisbord, S.: La comunicación pública: mutaciones e interrogantes. Nueva sociedad 96–109 (2017)
6. Burson-Marsteller. Twitter is the prime social media network for world leaders. In: PR Newswire (2017). https://www.prnewswire.com/news-releases/twitter-is-the-prime-soc ial-media-network-for-world-leaders-300466300.html. Accessed 4 Apr 2024
7. Chhabra, R.: Twitter Diplomacy: A Brief Analysis. Observer Research Foundation (2020)
8. Vasist, P.N., Chatterjee, D., Krishnan, S.: The polarizing impact of political disinformation and hate speech: a cross-country configural narrative. Inf. Syst. Front. **26**(2), 663–688 (2023)
9. Gupta, M., Dennehy, D., Parra, C.M., Mäntymäki, M., Dwivedi, Y.K.: Fake news believability: the effects of political beliefs and espoused cultural values. Inf. Manag. **60**, 103745 (2023)
10. Directorate-General for External Policies of the Union (European Parliament), Colomina, C., Sánchez Margalef, H., Youngs, R., Jones, K.: The Impact of Disinformation on Democratic Processes and Human Rights in the World. Publications Office of the European Union, Brussels (2021)
11. Lozano, J.S.: Petro, un presidente que 'tuitea' mucho, pero con poca estrategia. In: Contexto (2024). https://contextomedia.com/petro-un-presidente-que-tuitea-mucho-pero-con-poca-est rategia/. Accessed 10 Apr 2024
12. Cortés, S., Contreras, C: Petro: radiografía de un presidente tuitero. In: La Silla Vacía (2023). https://www.lasillavacia.com/historias/silla-nacional/petro-radiografia-de-un-presid ente-tuitero/. Accessed 11 Jun 2023
13. bcwtwiplomacy. 2022 Top 50 World Leader Power Ranking. In: Twiplomacy. (2022). https:// www.twiplomacy.com/top-50-world-leader-power-ranking. Accessed 7 Mar 2024

14. Blassing, S., Ernst, N., Engesser, S., Esser, F.: Populism and social media popularity: how populist communication benefits leaders on Facebook and Twitter. In: Taras, D., Davis, R. (eds.) Power Shift? Political Leadership and Social Media, pp. 97–111. Routledge, Abingdon (2020)

15. Milli, S., Carroll, M., Wang, Y., Pandey, S., Zhao, S., Dragan, A.: Engagement, user satisfaction, and the amplification of divisive content on social media. Knight First Amend. Inst. (2024)

16. Jungherr, A.: Analyzing Political Communication with Digital Trace Data: The Role of Twitter Messages in Social Science Research. Springer, Cham (2015). https://doi.org/10.1007/978-3-319-20319-5

17. Sádaba, T.: Origen, aplicación y límites de la "teoría del encuadre" (framing) en comunicación. Commun. Soc. (Formerly Comunicación y Sociedad) **14**, 143–175 (2001)

18. Goffman, E.: Frame Analysis: An Essay on the Organization of Experience. Harvard University, Cambridge (1974)

19. Hurtíková, H.: Framing Theory in the Field of Political Communication: Theoretical and Methodological Conceptualization. Contemp. Eur. Stud. 27–44 (2013)

20. Ardèvol-Abreu, A.: Framing theory in communication research. Origins, development and current situation in Spain. Rev. Latina Comun. Soc. **70**, 423–450 (2015)

21. Tuchman, G.: Making News: A Study in the Construction of Reality. Free Press, New York (1978)

22. Entman, R.M.: Framing: toward clarification of a fractured paradigm. J. Commun. **43**, 51–58 (1993)

23. Entman, R.M., Matthes, J., Pellicano, L.: Nature, sources, and effects of news framing. In: The Handbook of Journalism Studies (2009)

24. Mercado Sáez, M.T.: Diseño metodológico para el análisis del tratamiento informativo de las políticas energéticas en España y participación de organizaciones sociales. Universidad de Valladolid. Facultad de Ciencias Sociales, Jurídicas y de la Comunicación (2013)

25. Matthes, J.: Framing politics: an integrative approach. Am. Behav. Sci. **56**, 247–259 (2012)

26. Németh, R.: A scoping review on the use of natural language processing in research on political polarization: trends and research prospects. J. Comput. Soc. Sci. **6**, 289–313 (2023)

27. Kubin, E., von Sikorski, C.: The role of (social) media in political polarization: a systematic review. Ann. Int. Commun. Assoc. **45**, 188–206 (2021)

28. Oddo, J.: War legitimation discourse: representing 'Us' and 'Them' in four US presidential addresses. Discourse Soc. **22**, 287–314 (2011)

29. Jungherr, A.: Twitter in Politics: A Comprehensive Literature Review (2014)

30. Nguyen, J.: Politics and the Twitter revolution: a brief literature review and implications for future research. Soc. Netw. **7**, 243–251 (2018)

31. Darius, P., Stephany, F.: "Hashjacking" the debate: polarisation strategies of Germany's political far-right on Twitter. In: Weber, I., Darwish, K.M., Wagner, C., Zagheni, E., Nelson, L., Aref, S., Flöck, F. (eds.) SocInfo 2019. LNCS, vol. 11864, pp. 298–308. Springer, Cham (2019). https://doi.org/10.1007/978-3-030-34971-4_21

32. Pérez Curiel, C.: Political influencers/leaders on Twitter. An analysis of the Spanish digital and media agendas in the context of the Catalan elections of 21 December 2017. In: KOME, pp 88–108 (2020)

33. Esteve-Del-Valle, M.: Homophily and polarization in Twitter political networks: a cross-country analysis. Media Commun. **10**, 81–92 (2022)

34. Scacco, J.M., Wiemer, E.C.: The President Tweets the Press: President-Press Relations and the Politics of Media Degradation. In: Taras, D., Davis, R. (eds.) Power Shift? Political Leadership and Social Media, pp. 17–32. Routledge, Abingdon (2020)

35. Maurer, P., Diehl, T.: What kind of populism? Tone and targets in the Twitter discourse of French and American presidential candidates. Eur. J. Commun. (2020). https://doi.org/10.1177/0267323120909288

36. Waisbord, S., Amado, A.: Populist communication by digital means: presidential Twitter in Latin America. Inf. Commun. Soc. **20**(9), 1330–1346 (2017)

37. Flew, T., Iosifidis, P.: Populism, globalisation and social media. Int. Commun. Gaz. **82**, 7–25 (2020)

38. Álvarez-Peralta, M., Rojas-Andrés, R., Diefenbacher, S.: Meta-analysis of political communication research on Twitter: methodological trends. Cogent. Soc. Sci. **9**, 2209371 (2023)

39. Díez NL, López-López PC, Oñate P, Blasco-Blasco O: Emociones Y Polarización De Las Comunidades Digitales En América Latina: Elecciones Presidenciales 2018–2019. 182–210 (2023)

40. Elo, S., Kyngäs, H.: The qualitative content analysis process. J. Adv. Nurs. **62**, 107–115 (2008)

41. Krippendorff, K.: Metodología de análisis de contenido: teoría y práctica. Paidós Ibérica (1990)

42. Duarte Sandoval, L.: El año de los 5.650 trinos de Petro: estos son los datos de su actividad en Twitter. El Espectador (2023)

Correction to: The Spread of Anti-vaccination Memes on Facebook

Aleksi Knuutila, Anna George, Jonathan Bright, Kate Joynes-Burgess, and Philip Howard

Correction to:
Chapter 6 in: M. Preuss et al. (Eds.): *Disinformation in Open Online Media*, LNCS 15175, https://doi.org/10.1007/978-3-031-71210-4_6

The book was published with a missing author's name in chapter 6. The missing author is "Kate Joynes-Burgess" and she should have been mentioned as 4th author. This has been corrected in the corresponding chapter accordingly.

The updated version of this chapter can be found at
https://doi.org/10.1007/978-3-031-71210-4_6

Author Index

A
Abbasi, Mahdis   16
Ahrens, Maximilian   32
Aliahmadi, Mohammadhadi   16
Alizadeh, Meysam   16

B
Baghshahi, Zahra   16
Bright, Jonathan   86

C
Ceolin, Davide   70

D
Dehghani, Shirin   16
Dierickx, Laurence   1

E
Ebrahimi, Sarvenaz   16

F
Fromm, Jennifer   101

G
George, Anna R.   32
George, Anna   86
González-Méndez, María José   131
Gronert, Kim Henrik   101
Gruzd, Anatoliy   46

H
Howard, Philip   86

J
Joynes-Burgess, Kate   86
Jung, Anna-Katharina   101

K
Kloth, Niklas   131
Knuutila, Aleksi   86

L
Lindén, Carl-Gustav   1

M
Mai, Philip   46
McMahon, Michael   32
Mirzamojtahedi, Sara   16

O
Opdahl, Andreas L.   1

P
Pierrehumbert, Janet B.   32

R
Roitero, Kevin   70
Røysland, Kari Anne   101

S
Samei, Zeynab   16
Shahi, Gautam Kishore   101
Singh, Jaspreet   70
Soares, Felipe B.   46
Soprano, Michael   70

V
van Dalen, Arjen   1

Y
Yari, Sara   16

Z
Zahedivafa, Mohammadmasiha   16
Zare, Darya   16

M. Preuss et al. (Eds.): MISDOOM 2024, LNCS 15175, p. 147, 2024.
https://doi.org/10.1007/978-3-031-71210-4